LOST RAILWAYS

County Council

CUMBRIA LIBRARY SERVICES

This book is due to be returned on or before the last date above. It may be renewed by personal application, post or telephone, if not in demand.

C.L.18

COUNTRYSIDE BOOKS
NEWBURY, BERKSHIRE

First published 2008
© Gordon Suggitt 2008

COUNTRYSIDE BOOKS
3 Catherine Road
Newbury, Berkshire

To view our complete range of books,
please visit us at
www.countrysidebooks.co.uk

ISBN 978 1 84674 107 4

The cover picture shows 'Black 5' locomotive
no 45200 leaving Coniston station
and is from an original painting by
Colin Doggett

Produced through MRM Associates Ltd., Reading
Printed by Cambridge University Press

*All material for the manufacture of this book
was sourced from sustainable forests*

CONTENTS

ABBREVIATIONS

BR	British Railways (known as British Rail from late 1960s onwards)
C&W	Cockermouth & Workington Railway
C&WJ	Cleator & Workington Junction Railway
CK&P	Cockermouth, Keswick & Penrith Railway
DMU	Diesel multiple unit
FR	Furness Railway
L&C	Lancaster & Carlisle Railway
LMS	London, Midland & Scottish Railway
LNER	London & North Eastern Railway
LNWR	London & North Western Railway
LREC	Lakeside Railway Estates Company
M&C	Maryport & Carlisle Railway
NBR	North British Railway
NER	North Eastern Railway
S&D	Stockton & Darlington Railway
SD&LUR	South Durham & Lancashire Union Railway
TUCC	Transport Users Consultative Committee
WC&E	Whitehaven, Cleator & Egremont Railway

KEY TO MAPS

⚊⚊⚊ Coastline   Lake

⸺ Existing railway   − − − Disused railway

−+−+− Preserved railway | Halt

O Closed station   ● Open station
(selected stations only)

Station names are generally those in use
at the Grouping of 1923

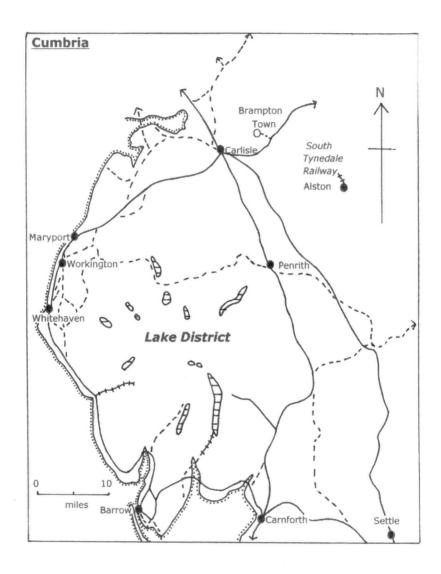

Introduction

Cumbria or the Lake District? Despite the appeal of the latter as a title, a glance at the introductory map shows why it proved unsuitable. Only five railway lines were built into the mountainous interior, with access to or near only four of the area's twelve major lakes. In addition three of these five survive, though only one as a part of the national rail network. As the other two comprise a narrow gauge survivor and (in part) a standard gauge preservation scheme, they have been included in this book, alongside the additional closed lines of the broader area, plus a further preserved railway. In passing, it is worth noting three reasons why there were so few lines built in the Lake District proper.

Firstly, there was the opposition to such schemes by those anxious to preserve the area's 'natural beauty'. This was led in the 1840s by the poet William Wordsworth, and then by various groups that combined in 1883 to form the Lake District Defence Society. Secondly, there were the difficulties posed by the terrain, for example, the climb to almost 1,200 ft above sea level required for the Braithwaite & Buttermere Railway proposed in 1882. Thirdly, the perceived lack of economic returns from such projects led to their abandonment, including the refusal of the LNWR to work the proposed Ambleside Railway of 1886, and the failure of schemes for Light Railways linking Coniston with Elterwater and with Greenodd on the Lake Side branch. It is the last of these three factors that played a major part in the decline of many lines that were built in the broader area.

So what is this larger 'Cumbria' area? Basically the post-1974 administrative area of Cumbria has been adhered to, comprising the 'old' counties of Cumberland and Westmorland, plus the Furness District of Lancashire and a small area of the former West Riding of Yorkshire, chiefly around Sedbergh. This gives a total of around 25 closed lines that at some point had had scheduled passenger services. However, this larger area still includes a mountainous core that acted as a barrier between many of the area's railways and the rest of the national network. Barrow, for instance, gained its first railway in 1846, but this remained isolated until the line was opened to Whitehaven in 1850, and it was another seven years before the completion of a direct link to the West Coast Main Line at Carnforth. Only on the area's eastern side were there lines of some of the major companies, the Midland and the North Eastern, and beyond Carlisle the North British and Caledonian companies. Elsewhere, despite absorptions by the LNWR, local interests predominated, with the Furness, Cleator & Workington Junction, Cockermouth, Keswick & Penrith and Maryport & Carlisle companies all remaining independent until the Grouping of 1923.

It is this profusion of different companies that helps give a rich variety to the area's closed lines. In length these varied from the 1¼ miles of the branch to Brampton Town, to the 30¾ miles of the Cockermouth–Penrith line, while passenger services ranged from the Pullman cars on the North British 'Waverley Route' to a single passenger coach added to workmen's trains on the branch to Lowca. There were also specials to convalescent homes, to ferry terminals and to schools, and even a service that continued to be horse-drawn until just before the First

World War. However, it is with a Furness Railway branch in the south-eastern corner that coverage begins, and then continues clockwise round the fringes of the Lake District to a finish just within present-day Yorkshire.

Gordon Suggitt

ACKNOWLEDGEMENTS

I would like to acknowledge the help and resources provided by libraries in Cumbria and elsewhere in North West England. I wish also to thank individually Leslie Oppitz for the use of his photo collection, Cliff Glover and Jack Dawson for the use of their reminiscences, and Mike Clark for his help with loco identification. Lastly, I am as ever especially grateful to my wife Jen for her help and encouragement, and particularly for her time and care over checking the text.

1
South Lakes and Barrow

Arnside–Hincaster Junction
The Lake Side branch
The Lakeside & Haverthwaite Railway
The Conishead Priory branch
The Piel branch
Barrow's closed stations
The Coniston branch

The fine station building at Ulverston still survives but the lines to Lake Side and Conishead Priory are amongst the area's lost railways. (Lens of Sutton Association)

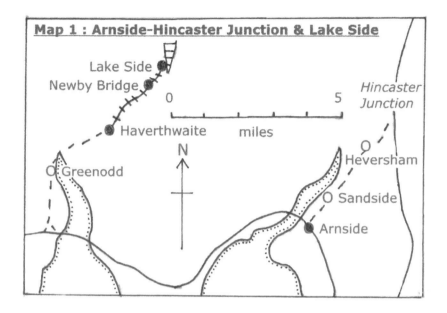

Map 1 : Arnside–Hincaster Junction & Lake Side

Arnside–Hincaster Junction

The Furness Railway (FR), described as 'the leading railway company in the Lake Counties', was an independent network of almost 120 miles at the Grouping of 1923, when it became part of the LMS. Its beginnings were modest, with a main line from Dalton to Barrow, and branches to Kirkby and Piel. This original 15-mile system was completely isolated from any other railway when it opened in 1846. Even its link to the West Coast Main Line at Lancaster was promoted and built by a separate company, the Ulverstone & Lancaster Railway, although worked by the FR from the start in 1857 and absorbed five years later. This main line through Ulverston and Barrow and on to Whitehaven remains in use today, but all the branches from it in the South Lakes and Barrow area were closed. The easternmost of these was built to link the main line at Arnside to the LNWR's West Coast Main Line at Hincaster Junction, 3¾ miles south of Oxenholme.

A distant view of the station at Sandside, as seen in the early 20th century. (Author's collection)

The first scheme for this branch was promoted by the independent Furness & Yorkshire Union Railway in 1864, for a link from Arnside to Kirkby Lonsdale as part of a cross-country project aimed at reaching the East Coast Main Line. This was opposed by the LNWR, which did agree to the FR taking over the scheme and modifying it to only reach Hincaster Junction. An Act for this was obtained in 1867 and the 5¼-mile single-track line opened nine years later, despite the objections of local landowner George Wilson. These led to several clauses in the line's Act and the construction of its two best features – the 26-arch Beela Viaduct and the chalet-style station at Sandside, designed by local architects Paley and Austin. A second station was later opened at Heversham in 1890.

The line was built to shorten the route for coke trains from South Durham to Barrow by avoiding a reversal at Carnforth, though it appears these soon reverted to the latter route. It wasn't until the First World War, when Carnforth was unable to cope with the

Ex-LMS Fairburn 2-6-4T no 42238 waits on the Hincaster spur at Arnside station in 1961. (Author's collection)

volume of traffic, that this trade returned. There were also some long-distance passenger trains, including through carriages from the NER on a Newcastle–Barrow service between 1905 and 1911. A later service continued in the form of the Durham–Ulverston trains up to the closure of the Stainmore Route in 1962. After the Grouping in 1923 there were through holiday trains on summer Saturdays from Leeds and Bradford to Windermere, as well as coaches for Barrow detached at Oxenholme from Windermere workings originating at Willesden and Northampton!

However, it was local passenger workings that kept the line busy. These began in 1876 with a weekday service of five trains each way between Grange-over-Sands and Kendal. This service, known locally as the 'Kendal Tommy', was increased to six in the 1920s and continued until 1942. All the trains stopped at the two intermediate stations; Sandside was the more imposing but the smaller Heversham station, with only one platform, was probably

'Railway Ramblers' by the surviving platform at Heversham in 2006. (Author)

the more important. This was due to the nearby Heversham Grammar School, popular with pupils from Grange and Kendal who used the train morning and late afternoon. Interestingly, Heversham station only ever had one stationmaster, Thomas Walker, in its 51 years of traffic. These ended with the withdrawal of local passenger services on 4th May 1942. Coke trains bound for Barrow kept the line open until 1963, when the line closed north of Sandside. That section was lifted and Heversham station demolished three years later. Sandside station was replaced by a block of flats and once quarry traffic ended there in 1971 the remainder of the line closed.

Today the approximate route of the line can be followed along the shore from Arnside to Sandside although this is a sea defence replacement. Where the route swung inland through limestone cuttings, it provides a pleasant walk to the site of Sandside station. Some of the rest of the route can then be walked to Hincaster

The interior of the terminus at Lake Side station in 1960.
(Author's collection)

Junction although access is often difficult. One section no longer in existence is the former Beela Viaduct, demolished in the 1960s, although its southern embankment can still be visited.

The Lake Side branch

This line was unusual in that it was built for tourism, as well as small industrial enterprises close to its route. In 1847 the Kendal & Windermere Railway reached the hamlet of Birthwaite, which later became the resort of Windermere, and by 1850 there were four steamers on the lake ferrying tourists between Waterhead (Ambleside) and Newby Bridge. The FR was keen to tap into this lucrative tourist trade and its Board of Directors first discussed building a branch from its main line to Newby Bridge in 1847, but it was the 1860s before this materialised. By then the FR

Ex-LMS class 2MT 'Mogul' 2-6-0 no 46441 (now preserved on the East Lancashire Railway) brings a passenger train into Lake Side in August 1965, only a month before closure. (W.H. Foster)

had obtained an Act for a two-mile branch to Greenodd, and its extension to Newby Bridge was authorised in 1866. Two substantial bridges across the Leven were required, and two short tunnels near Haverthwaite, but from there the route kept close to the Leven up to Newby Bridge. However, this was not to be the terminus as the directors had decided that a mile-long extension to a deepwater quay at Lake Side (the usual spelling before preservation) would be preferable to using Newby Bridge's shallow channel.

The line as completed was just under eight miles from a triangular junction at Plumpton, east of Ulverston, with double track as far as Greenodd and then a single line apart from a passing loop at Haverthwaite. It opened in 1869, with the official opening ceremony on 1st June, when loco no 21 with four coaches passed cheering crowds at Greenodd and Haverthwaite to reach a temporary wooden station at Lake Side, where there were the usual speeches and refreshments. Only the station at Greenodd appears to have been ready for this date, with those at Haverthwaite and Lake Side officially opening three months later. All the stations were built using 'patent white bricks' with contrasting trimming of purple ones (although these weathered to the yellow and black respectively as seen today at Haverthwaite). Local residents considered these to be 'alien' to the Lake District, but they contributed to a striking design at Lake Side, with an imposing frontage dominated by a tall clock tower. Behind was a combined railway station and steamer pier, with a train shed over 200 ft long and a lakeside refreshment pavilion, its upper storey a verandah which was provided with glass screens when it was extended in 1906.

Despite the FR's hopes for the line, and its takeover of the Windermere Steam Yacht Company's fleet of steamships in 1872, tourism does not seem to have been important on the branch in the early years. However, in 1896 Alfred Aslett became the railway's General Manager, and set about promoting tourism as a replacement for the declining iron trade. Crucial in this were the tours using charabancs, steamships and railways, visiting as many as 'Six Lakes' at a cost of thirteen shillings, and including links with Blackpool and Fleetwood via Barrow's Ramsden Dock (see later). The years up to 1914 were the heyday of the branch's tourist traffic, with a steam railmotor in 1905 calling at an extra halt known as 'Newby Bridge Motor Car Platform'! The railmotor only ran for a season but the halt stayed in use until 1939. By then the branch was in decline; the rundown of nearby industries (the two gunpowder works closed in the 1930s) and less local traffic left it dependent on tourism, which was profitable only in the summer months. The steamship sailings became summer-only from 1920, the branch's passenger operations followed suit in 1938 and its two intermediate stations at Greenodd and Haverthwaite shut in 1946.

Under BR the road-rail-water tours were revived, particularly from Morecambe, but passenger numbers were down and the line was listed for closure in the Beeching Report. This was originally scheduled for spring 1965, but that year's summer season was completed before the last passenger train departed Lake Side at 7.45 pm on 5th September without any ceremony. Goods services to and from Haverthwaite lasted another nineteen months but ended in April 1967 following the closure of Backbarrow Iron Works. Later that year, an enthusiasts' special travelled to Lake Side – the last use of the line before preservation.

The Lakeside & Haverthwaite Railway

The prospect of buying and operating a relatively short branch leading from a still-operational line into a National Park had great appeal for enthusiasts. Even before the closure by BR in

A 1910 postcard view of Lake Side, with (from left) Furness Railway steam yachts 'Swift' and 'Teal', the cargo boat 'Raven' and the combined steamship/ railway terminus. (Author's collection)

In 2007 much of the former Furness Railway's pierside building still survived, seen here with a later MV 'Teal' built for the LMS in 1936. (Author)

late 1967, the Lakeside Railway Estates Company (LREC) had already been established to save the branch with a view to reopening it as a tourist line using steam traction. By early 1968 three steam locos had been purchased and were being stored at Carnforth depot, and a supporters' group, the Lakeside Railway Society, had been set up. However, after overcoming opposition from the Lake District Planning Board, the LREC was then faced with the loss of a large part of Haverthwaite station yard and sections of the trackbed due to improvements to the A590 road. The costs of the alternative – the road instead bridging the railway – were beyond the LREC, which withdrew from the reopening scheme and instead concentrated on the 'Steamtown' development at Carnforth.

In 1970 a new company was formed from the LREC, with the aim of saving the upper 3½ miles of the line – the Lakeside

Ex-War Department Austerity Hunslet 0-6-0ST 'Cumbria' by the well-preserved station building at Haverthwaite in July 2003. (Author)

Bagnall 0-6-0ST 'Princess', formerly at Preston Docks, at the water column by Haverthwaite West Tunnel. (Author's collection)

Restored Furness Railway 0-4-0 no 20 is the pride of the preservation society's locomotive collection. (Author)

& Haverthwaite Railway Company Ltd. Progress by the usual standards of railway preservation was rapid as BR approved the sale in May 1970 and in October locos and coaches were delivered to the line. In May 1971 the first steam-hauled work train ran on the branch, and, after the threat of a public enquiry had been averted, the line was reopened to the public two years later. On 2nd May 1973 the 'Railway Bishop', the late Eric Treacy (Bishop of Wakefield), cut the tape linking a Lake Windermere steamship to ex-BR class 4MT loco no 42085 (with no 42073) at the head of a special train.

The line now has a total of 22 locomotives on its stocklist, as compared to seven in 1971. Twelve of the current total are steam engines, mostly ex-industrial, but also including the two examples of BR class 4MT used for the opening ceremony, two ex-Great Western locos and, on loan from the Furness Railway Trust, FR no 20. This restored loco, built in 1863, is believed to be

The much reduced terminus at Lakeside, with only one platform currently in use. (Author)

the oldest working standard gauge steam locomotive in Britain. There are also nine diesel engines and a petrol one previously used at a factory near Kendal.

Regular daily services operate on the line from April to October, with six trains a day plus an extra at Spring Bank Holiday week and midsummer, for the eighteen-minute journey between Haverthwaite and Lakeside. The former station has been well restored to its former condition, while the halt at Newby Bridge, closed since 1939, was reopened for the resumption of services in 1973. Little remains of the original station at Lakeside, where the station building and offices, with a distinctive tower, were demolished after years of neglect by BR. The loss probably little concerns today's travellers on the preserved railway as the main attraction at Lakeside is the ease of transfer to the adjacent landing stage for the lake cruises. There was concern over the future of these in 1984 when they were sold off as part of the privatisation of BR, but the current owners, Windermere Lake Cruises, continue to operate two of the pre-Second World War steamers, now converted to motor vessels, and MV *Tern* built in 1891, in conjunction with the railway's timetable.

Although there are the usual 'Thomas and Friends' events, steam and diesel weekends and 'Santa Specials', as well as Pensioners' Days in May and October, it is the combination of rail and water transport that adds a unique dimension and attracts many more tourists than would normally travel to a rail preservation scheme. Such train trips with lake cruises hark back to the earlier road, rail and water excursions, especially the midsummer 'Victorian Evenings' using FR no 20 and MV *Tern*, and help keep the preserved line at the forefront of Lake District attractions.

A postcard view of Conishead Priory in use as a 'hydropathic hotel' in the early 20th century. (Author's collection)

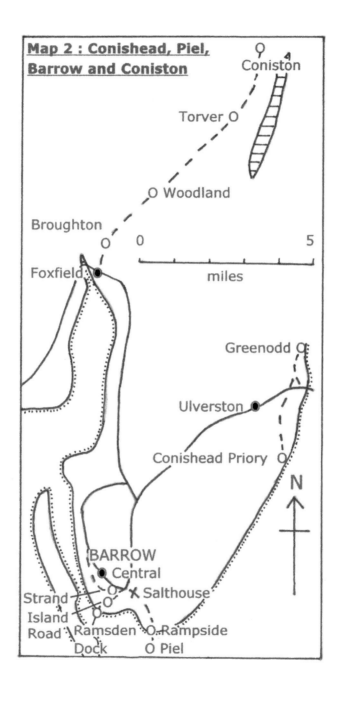

Map 2 : Conishead, Piel,
Barrow and Coniston

Coniston

Torver O

O Woodland

Broughton

Foxfield

0   5

miles

Greenodd O

Ulverston

Conishead Priory O

N

BARROW
Central

Strand
Island
Road   Ramsden   O Rampside
Dock   O Piel

Salthouse

One of the few later trains on the branch was the 'Furness Rail Tour' of 1961, here headed by ex-LMS class 4F 0-6-0 no 44347. (Author's collection)

The Conishead Priory branch

The FR main line west of Ulverston was built with tight curves and gradients as steep as 1 in 80 and 1 in 82, both over a mile in length, to reach a summit at almost 250 ft above sea level at Lindal. As this was followed by an equally steep descent towards Barrow, the whole section proved difficult for heavy freight trains, which at least in the 19th century usually required banking. In 1876 and 1881 the FR obtained Acts for a double-track loop line following the coast round from Ulverston to Barrow to provide an alternative. Only two miles of this were ever constructed, as far as Conishead Priory, plus a few hundred yards of earthworks, before the scheme was abandoned. The branch that was built opened in 1883, with two mixed trains each way from Ulverston to Priory station, a substantial building designed by the prominent

The line's only accessible remnant is this former swing bridge over the Ulverston Canal, still with its single track of rails. (Author)

Lancashire architects Paley and Austin, with a ticket office, ladies and general waiting rooms and an attached stationmaster's house. The Priory itself was a huge Gothic mansion built in the 1820s on the site of an Augustinian priory. Later in the 19th century it became a 'hydropathic hotel', with at least some visitors arriving by rail, although by 1901 it was advertising an omnibus service to and from Ulverston station instead.

By then the branch's passenger service had been reduced to only one train per day, although a halt had been added at North Lonsdale Crossing. Passenger trains were withdrawn as a wartime economy measure in 1917. The branch remained in use for freight, mostly to and from the North Lonsdale Ironworks by the Ulverston Canal, but most of the track was singled. In 1929 the Priory was purchased by the Durham Mineworkers' Welfare Committee for use as a convalescent home. By 1932, summer 'Special Passenger' trains ran on alternate Mondays (later Fridays) between Durham and Ulverston, via the Stainmore Route. On at least one occasion in 1936 LNER Sentinel steam railcar *North Briton* was used, which must have made for an uncomfortable journey over that distance. By the 1950s Ivatt class 2 and class 4 2-6-0 locos were used more, often with vintage pre-Grouping coaches. The service was maintained up to the summer of 1961, after which the closure of the Stainmore Route in January 1962 prevented a continuation. The ironworks closed in 1938 and its site was later used for a chemicals factory which opened in 1949. This kept the first mile of the route in use until 1994 but the remaining track was then lifted, and the entire branch is now difficult to trace, except for the bridge over the Ulverston Canal. After a period of neglect, the Priory has been restored by a Buddhist foundation, while its station is now a luxury holiday home frequented by pop stars and sports personalities. Not surprisingly, it is no longer accessible to the general public!

The Piel branch

Despite its name this branch terminated at Roa Island, three miles south-east of Barrow, although the original intention had been to reach Piel Island, almost a mile further south. In 1840, a London banker, John Abel Smith, bought both islands, intending to construct an embankment to Roa and a pier to Piel. Only the former was built, with a pier into deep water rather than to Piel, although called Piel Pier. Smith had large interests in the Preston & Wyre Railway and the town of Fleetwood which he intended to link to his purchases by steamer services. An Act for the embankment and pier was obtained in 1843, and the FR felt

Piel station in the early 20th century. (Lens of Sutton Association)

Today only the former Roa Island Hotel remains from the earlier scene. (Author)

Furness Railway loco no 44 was one of the class E1 type of 2-4-0 engines used on the branch around 1900. (Real Photographs)

forced to build a 2¼-mile branch from the main line at Roose to prevent Smith constructing his own competing line.

The 810 ft-long pier was not completed for the opening of the FR system on 3rd June 1846 and services on the branch did not begin until 24th August. Even then Smith's steamer was not ready, and the delays resulted in a dispute between Smith and the FR which lasted for the next seven years. In 1847–8 the FR even moved its steamer services to a pier at Barrow which could only be used at high tide. Eventually in December 1852 the pier and embankment at Roa were so severely damaged in a storm that Smith was glad to sell the lot to the FR for £15,000 in 1853. The FR repaired the damage and continued the sailings to Fleetwood, though these were reduced to summers-only from 1857. However, in 1862 the FR reached an agreement with the Midland which included the latter's transfer of its Isle of Man and

The trackbed at Rampside has been converted for use by cyclists, with the former station house at the left. (Author)

Belfast sailings from Morecambe to Piel. This led to the heyday of the pier and its railway, from 1867 to 1881. The Midland ran a 'boat train' from Leeds for the Isle of Man steamers, and through carriages from Leeds, with a connection from London, to fit in with the sailings to Belfast.

Ramsden Dock at Barrow was authorised in 1872 and completed seven years later. The Isle of Man steamers transferred to its berths on the Walney Channel from Piel in June 1881, following the provision of rail access to a new Ramsden Dock station. Four months later, the Belfast service also moved there, and Piel Pier was left disused until its demolition in 1891, but surprisingly this was not the end of the rail link. There appears to have been a branch line service from Barrow from the start, calling at an intermediate station called Concle, renamed Rampside in 1869. When the steamer service ended, a terminus was built on

Roa Island, although named Piel, with weekday services to and from Barrow, using a curve at Salthouse opened in 1873.

The original connection from the branch towards Ulverston, used by the boat trains, was removed in 1882, but the branch services, known locally as the 'Piel Nag', continued until 1936. In 1914 there were five trains to and from Barrow on weekdays, with an extra on Thursdays and two more on Saturdays. A halt was built on the Salthouse curve and opened in 1920, but the line was closed to all traffic on 6th July 1936. The embankment constructed by Smith now provides road access to Roa Island, while much of the branch's route on the mainland can be walked as part of the Cumbria Coastal Way. Rampside station buildings are still recognisable, but only the adjacent hotel marks the site of Piel station, with a stub of embankment leading from the island to where the pier once was.

Barrow's closed stations

When the FR built its first line into Barrow in 1846, the settlement was only a hamlet of some thirty cottages. Even so its jetties out into the navigable channel were shipping out around 40,000 tons of haematite (iron ore) a year from mines around Dalton and Lindale. This was the trade the FR aimed to tap with its line from Dalton to Barrow, although a passenger service was included to a single wooden platform station rustically named Barrow (Rabbit Hill)! The service seems to have been as primitive as the name suggests, with passengers allowed to travel in a converted sheep van and on Sundays only. A full service was later introduced, connecting with steamers at Piel Pier, but this was withdrawn at the end of the summer of 1846 due to the more pressing need to accommodate freight trains.

This problem was solved by doubling the central portion of the

Fine stonework on the only surviving former Furness Railway office building on the Rabbit Hill site, used in 2007 by a car sales firm. (J. Suggitt)

Barrow–Dalton main line, and, by 1850, the FR had carried 78,000 passengers. The Barrow station was rebuilt in stone in 1856, and in the 1860s major harbour developments converted the original channel into Devonshire and Buccleuch Docks. In conjunction with this, the FR converted the Rabbit Hill station into an engine shed and built a new Strand station, opened on 29th April 1863. An embankment built to link Barrow Island with the mainland was used for a diverted main line to Strand station, bypassing the Rabbit Hill site, which became the FR's offices and workshops. Strand station was enlarged in 1873, but by then there were plans for yet another main station for Barrow. This was Central station, located on a new loop line through the middle of the town, and opened in 1882.

By then, Barrow Island also had a station at Ramsden Dock,

Ramsden Dock station with an immaculate Furness Railway 4-4-0 locomotive. These were used for express working on the main line to Carnforth. (Cumbrian Railway Association)

named after the adjacent dock, although it served the deep water berth on Walney Channel. This was used by the Isle of Man and Belfast steamers after their transfer from Piel Pier. Its rail access was by an earlier (1873) rail link to a pier on Walney Channel, carried across the opening between Buccleuch and Ramsden Docks by an 80 ft swing bridge (replaced in 1907 by a roll lift bascule bridge). A further station was built on Barrow Island at Island Road, also known as Barrow Shipyard, with a single platform opened in 1899 for workmen's trains from Millom, Coniston and Grange-over-Sands. By 1915 it had a second platform and was in limited use by the general public, with Sunday school trips, excursions to Piel and Rugby League trains.

Barrow's stations did not do well in the 20th century; even Central, which has survived, was wrecked by bombing in 1941

The former Strand station is still a feature by the main road through Barrow. (Author)

Behind the frontage stands the one-time train shed with its two bricked-up entrances. (Author)

and not rebuilt until 1957. The original Rabbit Hill station was still in use as a carpenter's shed in 1960 but has since been demolished. Ramsden Dock station went into decline following the opening of Heysham Dock in 1904, even though the Midland agreed to keep some sailings from Barrow, which lasted until 1914. This left only occasional excursions, mainly to Blackpool, up to 1936, and Ramsden Dock station was demolished two years later. Island Road stayed open for workmen's trains until 1966, when the unsafe condition of the bascule bridge forced the closure of its access line. Only Strand remains of Barrow's closed stations, with both its original frontage and former train shed still standing.

The Coniston branch

The early development of the FR system included a 3½-mile branch from Kirkby to Broughton, opened in 1848 and built chiefly for shipments of copper ore from mines above Coniston. However, this still involved the use of barges on Coniston Water and horse-drawn transport at each end, so in 1849 a 3 ft 3 inch gauge rail link was proposed. This project was unsuccessful, but in 1857 it was revived as a standard gauge line to be built by the nominally independent Coniston Railway. Before it was completed, the Whitehaven & Furness Junction Railway, which had reached Broughton from the north in 1850, built a curve at Foxfield bypassing that station so that it was Foxfield that became the start of the Coniston branch.

The 8½-mile single-track line began passenger services without any ceremony on 18th June 1859, serving stations at Broughton (replacing the 1848 one), Woodland, Torver and Coniston. Surprisingly for a line intended for mineral shipments, freight services did not begin until the following year. However, the copper mines soon suffered from the effects of competition from

Torver station in April 1958, six months before closure. (Author's collection)

abroad, and the line became increasingly dependent on tourism. This was concentrated at Coniston, despite the location of its station which was convenient for the mines, but well away from the lake, and involved a steep climb from the village. The FR did its best, replacing the original station with an attractive chalet-style building in 1862, the year it absorbed the Coniston Railway. A third platform was added in 1896, plus a large 'tea pavilion' in 1905, but it was the lake that was the main attraction for visitors. Steamer services were begun by the FR in 1860, with the *Gondola* steam yacht. This was included in two of the 'Circular Tours of Lakeland' introduced by the FR in 1870. By 1906 the *Gondola* was carrying over 22,000 passengers annually, and two years later a much larger vessel, the *Lady of the Lake*, came into service.

The line was generally operated as a branch from Foxfield, initially with a service of four trains each way on weekdays and three on Sundays. Excursions were important from the start, the first running only three days after the line opened, with 430

Sunday school pupils among the 1,000 passengers in 30 carriages on a trip from Barrow. The years just before the First World War are regarded as the line's heyday, with eight weekday trains, plus an extra on Saturdays, and three on Sundays, in the summer of 1912. Surprisingly it was the August Bank Holiday weekend of 1915, almost a year after the outbreak of war, that was regarded as the line's busiest ever. Between 1905 and 1918 the FR used a steam railmotor on the branch, carrying 12 first class and 36 third class passengers, together with a four-wheeled trailer coach for an extra 34 in third class. Later both the LMS and BR operated push-pull trains for local services, although the terminus was provided with a turntable.

Both the line's isolated location in the south-west of the Lake District and the situation of Coniston station made the full development of its tourist potential difficult. After 1947 BR tried to remedy this, reintroducing the camping coaches set up by the LMS at Coniston, including the branch in its Holiday Runabout Area 2 (Lancs Coast and Lake District) and running twice-weekly summer excursions from Blackpool Central. However, the line remained primarily a local branch with under 250 passengers a day on its scheduled services except on summer Saturdays. By early 1957 there were rumours about closure, and in September the annual losses on the branch were put at over £16,000. Following official hearings and despite local objections, the end of passenger services was announced for October 1958, the first such closure in the Lake District. The last passenger train was the 8.52 pm from Foxfield on Saturday the 4th, again with little ceremony, although a placard reading 'Foxfield–Coniston. 41217. Oct 4/58 The End' was placed on the engine. There were about 100 passengers, including around 40 enthusiasts, some of whom are believed to have travelled back with the train which officially returned to Barrow 'empty'!

The former branch terminus at Coniston. (Courtesy of L. Oppitz)

Coniston's signal box and engine shed have also been demolished, but the footbridge was later rebuilt at Ravenglass. (Courtesy of L. Oppitz)

An early 20th-century view of Broughton station. (Courtesy of L. Oppitz)

Broughton station building still survives as two residences. (Author)

Goods traffic continued three times a week until 1962, after which the line was abandoned. It is still visible in places, although walkable for only half a mile south from the site of Coniston station. The handsome building was sadly demolished in 1968, with its only surviving remnant the footbridge which was re-erected at the narrow-gauge station at Ravenglass (see next chapter). The line's other stations at Broughton, Woodland and Torver all remain as residences, but the least likely survival is the steam yacht *Gondola*. While the *Lady of the Lake* was broken up in 1950, *Gondola* was converted into a houseboat, wrecked, and eventually submerged. After a successful £100,000 appeal it was rescued by the National Trust and restored by Vickers of Barrow for a return to service on the lake in 1980, well outlasting the railway that brought many of its early passengers.

2

La'al Ratty: the Ravenglass & Eskdale Railway

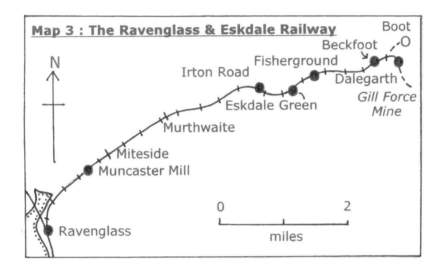

Map 3 : The Ravenglass & Eskdale Railway

Probably the area's best-known operational railway is also its smallest, at least in terms of gauge. The 15-inch Ravenglass & Eskdale Railway runs for 7 miles up the valley of the Esk from the small settlement of Ravenglass, the only coastal village within the Lake District National Park. It was first reached by rail in 1849, when the Whitehaven & Furness Junction Railway opened its line from Whitehaven. This was extended south to the FR in 1850 and absorbed by the latter company fifteen years later. Eskdale, like much of Western Cumbria, was rich in iron ore deposits, worked sporadically since Roman times. Modern working began early in the 19th century, but was handicapped by the cost of carriage over rough roads to the coastal railway. However, in 1872, the Whitehaven Iron Mines company promoted a Bill for a 'narrow gauge railway or tramway from the Eskdale Mines to Ravenglass', to be built and operated by the separate Ravenglass & Eskdale Railway Company.

A 3 ft gauge line was duly built and opened on 24th May 1875, linking Ravenglass to the village of Boot and Nab Gill mine, reached by an incline. Eighteen months later a passenger service began with three daily trains in summer, and two in winter, taking 45–60 minutes for the 210 ft climb to Boot. These called at single platform stations at Ravenglass, Irton Road, Eskdale Green, Beckfoot and Boot, with a halt at Muncaster. Two 0-6-0 tank engines were provided by Manning Wardle, *Devon* and *Nab Gill*, with two four-wheeled passenger coaches, although open wagons were also used. However, the ore deposits did not meet expectations and within six months of the line opening to passengers it was put into receivership.

Surprisingly this did not seem to affect the passenger services, which increased to five weekday trains (three on Sundays) in summer 1878. There were even attempts to expand the mining activities, with a new ¾-mile branch to Gill Force mine in the 1880s and sporadic workings at Nab Gill, but it was basically passengers (who reached a peak of over 32,000 in 1903) and local goods that kept the increasingly dilapidated line going into the 20th century. Eventually despite the formation of a new company, the Eskdale Railway Co, passenger services ended in 1908, and after various leases to mining companies, the 'Owd Ratty' line closed on 30th April 1913.

The First World War would seem the unlikeliest time for the line to be 'reborn' as 'La'al Ratty' but that is what happened in 1915. Over the previous ten years there had been a vogue for miniature railways, built to the tiny gauge of 15 inches, both in

0-6-0 'Devon' on the 3 ft gauge line at Boot around 1905. (Ravenglass & Eskdale Railway Co.)

The same location about twelve years later, with Bassett-Lowke's 4-6-2 'Colossus' on the 15 inch gauge track. (G.P. Abraham Ltd)

Britain and in Europe. An enthusiast, Robert Proctor Mitchell, and the engineer W.J. Bassett-Lowke had combined in various projects which largely came to an end due to the war. Somehow Proctor Mitchell heard of the Eskdale line, which was by then derelict, and negotiated for its lease with a view to conversion to a 15-inch gauge line. Work began in July 1915, before the agreement was signed, and by August the 'new' line had reached Muncaster Mill, followed by Irton Road in October. The official opening (to Beckfoot) took place on 20th April 1916, with Bassett-Lowke's 4-4-2 *Sans Pareil* (originally *Prins Olaf* from its pre-war exhibition days in Oslo) and seven passenger coaches also from Norway. Two more locos, *Katie* and *John Anthony* (renamed *Colossus*), soon arrived from the Duke of Westminster's estate railway at Eaton Hall, Cheshire, followed by *Ella* and *Muriel* from another private estate in 1917. These allowed the provision of passenger services similar to those in the 1870s, which seem to

The first 'River Mite', seen here at Eskdale Green in 1928, was built from the remains of 'Colossus', 'Sans Pareil' and 'Sir Aubrey Brocklebank'. (Ravenglass & Eskdale Railway Co.)

'River Esk', originally built for the line's stone quarry traffic, at Ravenglass in July 1962. (Author's collection)

have been well patronised, even in the middle of the war. They were even extended to Boot in 1917, possibly in conjunction with the reopening of Nab Gill mine, but the gradient proved too much for the Bassett-Lowke engines, and Beckfoot became the terminus once more in 1918.

Little changed in the 1918–1939 period except with regard to locos. *Katie* was sold in 1918, *Ella* withdrawn in 1926 and *Muriel* was rebuilt and renamed *River Irt* in 1928 (and is still operational today – the world's oldest 15 inch gauge loco). New engines were built in 1919 and 1923; the first of these, *Sir Aubrey Brocklebank*, only saw service until 1927, but parts of it were used, along with bits of *Sans Pareil* and *Colossus* (scrapped in 1926 and 1927 respectively) in the construction of *River Mite* in 1928. This too was scrapped in 1937, but the 1923 loco *River Esk* is still in use today. Regarding the line, the up-valley terminus was changed, first to

'Northern Rock', under the former Coniston station footbridge in its position at Ravenglass up to January 2004. (Author's collection)

Dalegarth Cottages on the former Gill Force branch in 1922, and finally to the present-day Dalegarth station by Eskdale's 'main' road in 1927. In a development important for the line's later history, quarries at Beckfoot were reopened in 1922, this time for the extraction of granite.

Passenger services ended with the outbreak of war in 1939 and did not restart until Whitsun 1946. Three years later the line was bought by Keswick Granite, together with the Beckfoot quarry. In 1953 the Keswick company closed down the quarry but continued to run the railway, which it attempted to sell in 1958. After two years the line was put up for auction and was bought for £12,000 by the Ravenglass & Eskdale Railway Preservation Society, which had been set up only a month previously. In 1961 an operating company, the Ravenglass & Eskdale Railway Co Ltd, was formed and has continued to run the line ever since, while

The second loco to be named 'River Mite', in service since 1967, at the rebuilt terminus at Dalegarth. (Author)

the society concentrates on fund-raising. Major improvements have included the rebuilding of Ravenglass station layout in 1966–67, followed by new buildings by 1983, the purchase of new locomotives *River Mite* in 1967 and *Northern Rock* in 1976 (the line's centenary), and the rebuilding of the Dalegarth terminus, officially opened in April 2007.

Today, despite its remote location, the line has around 125,000 visitors a year. Most take the full 35 minute journey to the terminus at Dalegarth and back. All the other original stations are still in use, except Boot, and there are additional stops at Muncaster Mill, closed in 1924 but reopened in 1967, and Fisherground, a mile west of Beckfoot, to serve a campsite. Trains run in every month of the year, the frequency ranging from weekends in November and December to sixteen every day from mid-July to the end of August. Almost all the services are steam-hauled by *River Irt, River Esk, River Mite* or *Northern Rock*, four pre-Christmas diesel weekends being the main exception.

Muscle-power is needed for 'River Mite' on the turntable at Dalegarth. (Author)

With operations now into a third century, this line through one of England's most beautiful valleys has been described as 'one of the great survivors' and remains a major attraction for tourists and enthusiasts alike.

3
Coal and Iron: the Whitehaven, Cleator & Egremont Railway

Mirehouse Junction–Moor Row–Sellafield
Moor Row–Marron Junction
Distington–Parton

Moor Row, seen here at a railtour visit in September 1954, was the hub of the WC&E system. Its shed had just closed, but two months previously nine locos had been allocated there. (Author's collection)

Mirehouse Junction–Moor Row–Sellafield

In 1849 the coast line north of Ravenglass was opened to Whitehaven, where it met the Whitehaven Junction line of 1847. Both these had been sponsored by Lord Lowther (later the 2nd Earl of Lonsdale), who was keen to add other lines to tap the mineral resources of the West Cumberland coalfield. This was dominated by high-grade iron ore rather than the coal, which was of poorer quality. The Whitehaven Iron & Steel Company had been set up in 1841 to exploit the iron ore reserves, opening the orefield's first iron works at Cleator the following year. In 1854 another Lonsdale-sponsored company, the Whitehaven, Cleator & Egremont Railway (WC&E) was incorporated. Its line left the coast route at Mirehouse Junction, a mile south of Corkickle station at Whitehaven, using a curving route to minimise gradients south and east to Moor Row near Cleator. Every single iron mine in the Cleator and Egremont area was eventually reached by a web of tracks from this point. From Moor Row, the WC&E built lines east to Frizington and south to Egremont. These opened for mineral traffic in January 1856, with passenger services from stations at Moor Row, Cleator Moor, Frizington and Egremont starting eighteen months later. These were originally to Bransty station at Whitehaven, but were soon switched to Corkickle following the imposition of a toll for trains passing through Whitehaven Tunnel. There was also a goods station at Crossfield, south of Cleator Moor, where the original station also became goods-only in 1866 as a 1¼-mile loop with a new passenger station was built further west to avoid subsidence on the older route.

The Mirehouse Junction–Moor Row section was double-tracked in 1863, and six years later the Egremont line was extended 7½ miles south through an intermediate station at Beckermet to

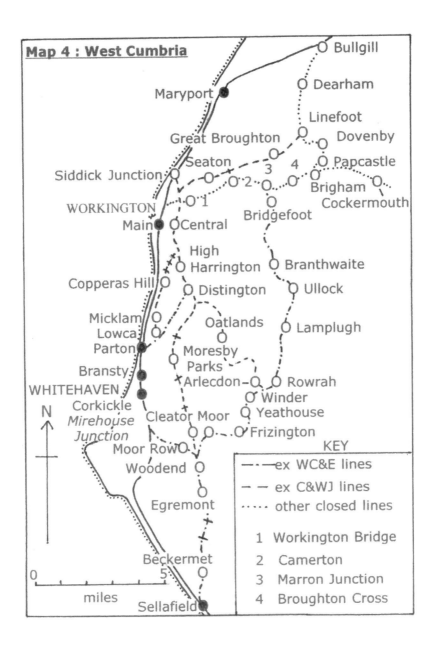

Map 4 : West Cumbria

KEY

—·—·—ex WC&E lines

— — ex C&WJ lines

······ other closed lines

1 Workington Bridge
2 Camerton
3 Marron Junction
4 Broughton Cross

The WC&E station, seen here in the early 20th century, was the larger of the two serving Cleator Moor. (Northern Historical Images)

Now all that is left at Cleator Moor is this striking design on the bridge over the original branch, now used as a cycleway. (Author)

0-6-0ST no 17 'Wastwater', seen here as Furness Railway no 108, was based at Moor Row around 1914 and was the last surviving ex-WC&E engine when scrapped by the LMS in 1925. (Author's collection)

the FR at Sellafield. A further station was added at Woodend in 1880, plus halts for iron mine workers at Beckermet Mines and St Thomas Cross Platform. The extension was jointly owned with the FR, which in partnership with the LNWR absorbed the WC&E in 1878. The LNWR then handled the line's passenger services, with, in 1922, eight to nine weekday trains from Whitehaven to Moor Row, most continuing to Egremont or Sellafield. However, passenger trains were infrequent and slow, taking 21 minutes between Moor Row and Sellafield, and the service did not survive the Depression, ending on 5th January 1935.

Cliff Glover worked as a cleaner at Moor Row engine shed in the 1940s and kept a record of the workings there. These were mostly freight but included workmen's trains from Workington and Whitehaven via Moor Row to Sellafield, which had resumed in 1940. They were sometimes worked by ex-FR engines including 0-6-0T no 11553 and 0-6-2T no 11628 (the last survivors of their respective classes). In the early 1940s, Cliff also recorded workmen's trains to Millom, and special passenger trains to that destination and to Carlisle. Between May 1946 and June 1947 there was a short-lived revival of the full passenger service at Moor Row, also Woodend, Egremont and Beckermet, and around that time Saturday specials ran from Moor Row to Workington Central, for 7d return, along with miners' outings from Moresby Parks to Seascale. As late as 1954 Moor Row could still be busy with passenger trains, as on 5th September, when at the time of the visit of the 'West Cumberland Rail Tour' there was also a Rugby League excursion from Egremont to Workington hauled by class 4F 0-6-0 no 44390, and its connection from Cleator Moor with 2-6-0 no 46457.

Workmen's trains continued to run from Moor Row to the nuclear plant at Sellafield until 1965, earning Egremont station a mention for closure in the Beeching Report. This was despite a proposal at the time to shut the coast line through Whitehaven, repeatedly closed by cliff falls especially along the stretch known to railwaymen as 'Avalanche Alley'. The plan was to reinstate passenger services through Egremont on the ex-WC&E route and on to Workington by the former C&WJ line (see next chapter). However, nothing came of this and only iron ore mines at Ullcoats and Beckermet kept the line open for freight, with final closure in stages from 1970. The last iron ore shipments (from Beckermet) were in 1980, while the Mirehouse Junction–Moor Row section retained a single track for another ten years. Now that stretch is part of the National Cycle Network route 72, while both the original and later routes through Cleator Moor are in use for route 71. Further south, only short stretches are in similar use, but a fine example of the line's stations survives at Woodend.

Woodend has a particularly fine example of a restored station building, here seen from the former platform side. (Author)

Moor Row–Marron Junction

The 1860s and 70s were a time of rapid expansion for the West Cumberland iron and steel industry following the development of the Bessemer process for steel-making in 1856. This led the WC&E to extend its Frizington branch, first 5¼ miles to Kidburngill in 1862, then four years later a further 6½ miles north to Marron Junction for access to Workington. Although this single-track line was primarily for iron ore and limestone, passenger services were soon introduced. Stations were opened at Eskett, Winder and Rowrah in 1864, and Wright Green (the name used at Kidburngill until 1901, when it became Lamplugh), Ullock, Branthwaite, Bridgefoot and Marron Junction in 1866. The line was difficult to work, especially with the climb to a summit

The simple station at Bridgefoot in the early years of the 20th century. (Author's collection)

at over 550 ft above sea level near Rowrah, and included a 1 in 44 gradient on a sharp curve in a wooded cutting near Yeathouse. From Rowrah northwards the route followed the Marron valley, requiring six crossings of the river. The line also had problems with the subsidence caused by iron ore mining, with a deviation needed at Eskett in 1872, involving ¾ mile of new track and a new station at Yeathouse. The original Eskett station became a goods depot which remained in use until 1931.

The line was doubled throughout by 1873, making it easier to fit the sparse passenger services from Whitehaven and Moor Row to Workington in amidst the flow of freight trains (though much of it was later singled as traffic declined). The station at Marron Junction was closed in 1897, and the junction's east curve taken out five years later. The few passengers for Cockermouth then had to change at Camerton, although a single southbound train from

Cockermouth, with a reversal at Marron Junction, continued to run early in the 20th century. By 1922, passenger trains over the whole route were down to three to four on weekdays, with another four each way over the Moor Row–Rowrah section. These only lasted until 1931, the last scheduled passenger trains running on 11th April. In 1938, freight traffic over the line to Marron Junction was boosted by the transfer of limestone shipments from Rowrah, with the closure of the line to Distington (see next chapter). However, by 1954 these had been switched to run via Moor Row and the line north to Marron Junction went out of use. The SLS/ MLS 'West Cumberland Railtour' is thought to have been the last train over this northern stretch before the track was lifted in 1964. Limestone trains continued from Rowrah to Moor Row until 1978, when this section closed completely. It is now part of cycle route no 71, and station houses survive at Frizington,

The 1954 railtour at Rowrah, en route for Marron Junction.
(Author's collection)

Winder still has its former station house and a surviving platform. (Author)

Winder (together with its platform) and Rowrah. Further north the trackbed has gone out of use, though still visible in places, while the former station house at Wright Green/Lamplugh is now a holiday cottage.

Distington–Parton

This appears detached from the rest of the WC&E system but was the western end of the Gilgarran branch, built from the Moor Row–Marron Junction line at Ullock to the station and iron works at Distington and opened in 1879. This was operational as a goods-only line until closure in 1929, but its western extension, from Distington to Parton on the coast line and also opened in 1879, managed a short-lived passenger service. Between June 1881 and December 1883 two trains a day ran each way between Whitehaven, Parton and Distington, where the service

A view of Distington unusually busy with the 1954 railtour's passengers. The Parton branch platform can be seen on the left with the wagons. (Author's collection)

An early 20th-century view of Parton at the other end of the branch. (Lens of Sutton Association)

had its own platform, and there was a revival for a mere eleven months in 1913–14. During its short life this must have been an interesting ride, with a descent of 250 ft in 2½ miles to the coast. No intermediate stations were provided but after closure to regular passenger trains, a workmen's service ran to Parton (or Lowca Pit) Halt 100 yards up the branch until 1929. Closure of most of the branch to freight followed three years later, but the westernmost ¾ mile stayed in use for access to Harrington No 10 colliery at Lowca until 1973. This section, including the site of the halt, is the only part of the one-time passenger route not now available as a cycle route, as the remaining 2¼ miles to Distington have been converted for use by cyclists, walkers and horse-riders.

4

Ironmasters' Lines: the Cleator & Workington Junction Railway

Cleator Moor–Siddick Junction
Calva Junction–Linefoot
Distington–Arlecdon
The Harrington & Lowca Light Railway

The headquarters of the C&WJ were at Workington Central, upstairs in the station building on the left. (Lens of Sutton Association)

Cleator Moor–Siddick Junction

The Cleator & Workington Junction Railway (C&WJ) was established as a direct response to increases in the freight rates charged by the LNWR and W&CE. In 1875 the 'ironmasters' of West Cumberland, led by the Lords Lonsdale and Leconfield and Henry Frazer Curwen, promoted a Bill for a line from the WC&E at Cleator Moor to the LNWR (formerly Whitehaven Junction Railway) at Siddick north of Workington. It is likely that they would have preferred to avoid the LNWR altogether and link instead with the Maryport & Carlisle, but were deterred by the hilly terrain north of the Derwent valley. As it was the route was far from ideal, involving 11½ miles of double track almost entirely on a gradient of 1 in 70, as the land rose to 460 ft above sea level at Moresby Parks. Most of the industries and settlements were already served by the W&CE and LNWR, and the line was forced to run through sparsely populated country, with the many small furnaces usually requiring branches. Passenger trains were provided from the line's opening as far north as Workington in October 1879, starting at the station at Moor Row opened by the WC&E in 1857, and calling at the C&WJ's separate station at Cleator Moor, plus ones provided at Moresby Parks, Distington, High Harrington and Workington. At the latter's Central station (used as a location in the 1939 film *The Stars Look Down*) the company built a rather grim two storey building for its headquarters, with offices and boardroom on the upper level. Workmen's halts were also built at industrial locations; at least one of these, Moresby Junction, was in public use early in the 20th century. In 1880 the service was extended north across a four-span lattice deck girder bridge over the River Derwent to Siddick, where a junction station was built on the coast route between Workington and Maryport.

High Harrington, one of the C&WJ main line's intermediate stations, seen after closure in 1931. (Lens of Sutton Association)

Passenger traffic on this 'main line' was essentially local and secondary to freight, as was the case over the whole C&WJ system which eventually totalled 32 miles (including minerals-only branches). In 1922, the last year of operation, over 800,000 tons of freight (less than half the peak year of 1909's total) brought receipts of £84,349 as against only £6,570 from passenger fares. Nevertheless, by 1919, Workington Central station had thirteen weekday passenger trains departing to various destinations on the C&WJ system, rising to eighteen on Saturdays. The C&WJ remained independent although largely worked by the FR, but in the Grouping it was absorbed by the LMS, ending its existence with a 'grand farewell dinner for 150 officials and staff' at Workington's Central Hotel after the last shareholders' meeting on 28th February 1923. The 'main line' had seen more passenger services than the rest of the C&WJ system, with five Moor Row–Siddick trains on weekdays in 1922, but these ended in April 1931, leaving only freight traffic and the occasional diversion from the

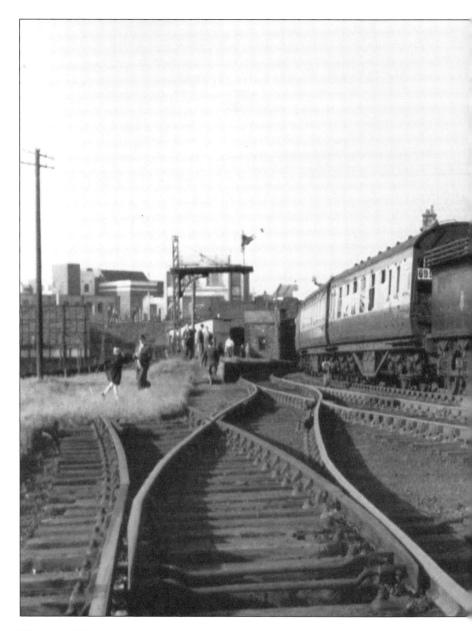

The 1954 'West Cumberland Rail Tour' at the Workington Central site, with ex-Furness Railway 0-6-0 no 52501. (Author's collection)

This modern footbridge has been built on the piers of the C&WJ crossing of the Derwent at Workington. (Author)

coast line, plus excursions. These continued until 1963, when the ex-C&WJ main line shut south of Harrington Junction, followed by the remainder two years later. South of Distington, the 7-arch viaduct at Keekle and the station house at Moresby Parks survive, but the route has disappeared completely in places. Only the first ¼ mile at Cleator Moor is used as a cycleway, and a similar stretch is a footpath at Moresby Parks. To the north the opposite applies as almost the whole length of former trackbed between Distington and Siddick is in use as a cycle track. Here, however, nothing is left of the stations, and only the piers of the bridge over the Derwent at Workington survive, now carrying a footbridge built in 1975.

Calva Junction–Linefoot

The C&WJ still sought to replace its connection with the LNWR at the northern end of its main line. The original aim had been to reach Maryport, but in 1883 this was replaced by a Bill for a line from Calva Junction, about a mile north of Workington Central station, to the Solway Junction Railway at Brayton. However, in a Bill three years later it abandoned much of this route in favour of a connection from Calva Junction to the Maryport & Carlisle Derwent branch at Linefoot (see Chapter 6). This shorter 6½ mile line, sometimes referred to as the C&WJ's 'Northern Extension', was still difficult to work as the earlier Cockermouth & Workington Railway had taken the easier route via the Derwent valley (see Chapter 5). The C&WJ was forced to cross hillier country to the north, rising to 250 ft above sea level and with gradients of 1 in 50 in places. It opened for freight in 1887 and, the following year, a limited passenger train service was introduced between Workington and Seaton, at the end of the double-track section of the branch. This ended in 1897, but resumed ten years later, and for two months in 1908 the passenger service was extended to the former goods depot at Great Broughton and on to Linefoot.

Around this time the line was used for excursions from Cleator Moor and Workington to Carlisle, as well as for coke trains from Durham to West Cumberland. By 1919 the passenger services to Seaton were down to two Saturdays only trains each way, and ended altogether three years later. The Grouping of 1923 removed the need for an alternative through route for freight, and when its outlet via the Derwent branch shut in 1935 the Calva Junction–Linefoot line was cut back to Buckhill Colliery. When this too closed in 1939, its site became used for a military establishment which kept the track open from Calva Junction, along with ¾ mile of the former C&WJ main line south from Siddick Junction. This allowed railtours to access the branch as far as the military depot in the late 1960s, but the depot and its rail access closed in 1992. The late closure helps to explain the availability of the route through Seaton and past Camerton for a cycleway, while

The former Seaton station in the 1950s, when the line was still in use for the Broughton Moor military depot. (Author's collection)

The station at Seaton has gone but the former line still has two road bridges, complete with racing cyclists! (Author)

the easternmost mile of former trackbed is now a road giving better access to Little Broughton.

Distington–Arlecdon

This was the stretch of the C&WJ's Oatlands (or Rowrah) branch that carried passengers, albeit briefly and always secondary to freight movements. Better known as 'Baird's Line' after a noted Scottish 'ironmaster', the railway was built south from Distington to Rowrah, where it met the Rowrah & Kelton Fell Mineral Railway. This 3½ mile freight-only branch opened in 1877 to exploit limestone and iron ore in the area close to Ennerdale Water. It was originally connected to the WC&E, just west of Rowrah station, but had close links with the C&WJ, which

The C&WJ initially used Furness Railway engines, but for this branch and those to coastal steelworks a total of ten locos were purchased, including 0-6-0ST no 10 'Skiddaw Lodge' ordered in 1917. (Real Photographs)

A view of Oatlands station, probably disused but still with nameboards on the platform and signalbox. (Lens of Sutton Association)

agreed to build a connection to Distington, giving much more direct access to Workington than the WC&E lines. However, this was only achieved with a winding route (6¾ miles between Distington and Rowrah as against a direct distance of 4½ miles) and by crossing hilly country rising to 600 ft above sea level, with gradients as steep and lengthy as 1 in 44 over a 2-mile stretch.

The single-track line opened for mineral traffic in 1882, with a passenger service the following year. Details of this are sketchy, but it appears to have been initially from Workington to a solitary station at Oatlands. A second station opened at Arlecdon, a mile west of Rowrah, around the same time but only for workmen's trains. The first Oatlands service lasted only five months, but it was revived between 1888 and 1892, and again in 1909. Three years later it was extended to Arlecdon. Just how much of a service this was is unclear, but it is unlikely to have ever been more than a couple

The former station building at Arlecdon today. (Author)

of trains on Saturdays, and perhaps for a time on Wednesdays as well. Certainly, by 1919, there was a single passenger train each way as far as Oatlands on Saturdays only (the service to Arlecdon having ended in 1916), and even this finished in 1922.

By then the mineral railway's iron ore traffic had ended, and only the limestone shipments continued from its western end. These kept 'Baird's Line' open until 1938, when a connection was put in from the quarries to the WC&E at Rowrah, allowing the limestone to be taken out via Marron Junction (and later via Moor Row). In 1939 the line was abandoned, apart from ½ mile of track at Arlecdon kept as a siding until 1980. This early closure helps to explain why so little of it is walkable today, with only a short stretch into the former quarries at Rowrah in use as part of cycle route 71. Elsewhere the route has largely disappeared; the only significant remnant is the former station building at Arlecdon.

The Harrington & Lowca Light Railway

This short 2¼-mile line is usually included with the C&WJ, although it was set up as a separate concern and its complex origins have more to do with freight workings. A mineral railway, originally named the Lowca Tramway, ran from the harbour at Harrington to Lowca colliery. In 1877 this was joined above the harbour by a C&WJ branch from its main line at Harrington Junction. This made it feasible to run trains from Workington Central and, following the successful introduction of workmen's services in April 1912, an application was made for a Light Railway Order which permitted a passenger service with basic facilities. This was begun by the CW&J in June 1913 and continued until 1926, usually with a single FR coach attached to the workmen's

The first passenger train at Lowca in 1913, with FR 0-6-0 no 12 built by Sharp Stewart in 1874. (Cumbrian Railways Association)

The harbour at Harrington was the destination of the original mineral line, with the section used for the passenger service above the cliffs in the distance. (Author)

carriages for 'ordinary' passengers. Initially, one train daily ran from Seaton on the Calva Junction–Linefoot branch, but for the final four years all began at Workington Central. Basic stations, really just shelters, were built on the C&WJ stretch at Harrington Church Road Halt and Rosehill Archer Street, and on the Light Railway proper at Copperas Hill, Micklam and Lowca. In 1922 there were three to four weekday trains each way, which must have provided an exciting journey as the line had the steepest gradient in Britain worked by conventional passenger trains. This was almost 300 yards of 1 in 17 immediately south of the Rosehill station. When the rails were slippery, trains had to reverse back from the station to get a good run at the climb! Despite this hazardous journey, the service, known locally as the 'Rattler', was popular especially for Saturday trips to the market at Workington.

This remnant at the former Copperas Hill station is all that is left of the line's structures. (Author)

In 1923 the LMS introduced 'Bus Trains', manned by travelling ticket inspectors, but the service could not compete with road competition and ended in 1926, followed by the workmen's trains three years later. After closure to passengers, the line continued in use for freight up to May 1973, with the last working on the 26th using two diesel electric engines belonging to the British Steel Corporation. These had hauled brake van trips, popular with enthusiasts in the late 1960s and early 70s, although the Border Railway Society's *Furnessman* railtour in 1969 also included an appearance by NCB Hunslet 0-6-0 Austerity saddle tank *Amazon*. Now over a mile of the former Light Railway section is part of the Cumbria Coastal Way. This continues to Harrington Harbour on the original mineral line's trackbed, allowing walkers to sample the even steeper 1 in 15 descent to the harbour as well as the infamous stretch once used by passenger trains. Little else is left of the light railway, except for the crumbling ruin of the 'station' building at Copperas Hill.

5
Across the Fells

The Cockermouth & Workington Railway
Cockermouth–Keswick–Penrith

Holiday traffic to Keswick, with two Ivatt class 2MT locos on a Whit Monday 1963 excursion from Carlisle in the Greta gorge. (Author's collection)

The Cockermouth & Workington Railway

Although this line later became part of a through route, it began as an 8½-mile branch inland from Workington to the market town of Cockermouth. Incorporated in 1845, the Cockermouth & Workington Railway (C&W) opened its single-track line two years

Workington Bridge station, with the town and two rail crossings of the Derwent in the left background. (Lens of Sutton Association)

later, principally to serve collieries around Camerton. Passenger services were included, but initially with only one engine and enough carriages for a single train. The line's route, shown on Map 4, followed a level course along the valley floor of the River Derwent, with five crossings of the river by iron spans on stone piers. Stations were provided at Workington Bridge, Camerton, Broughton Cross and Brigham before the terminus on the western outskirts of Cockermouth, where a small covered station was squeezed in amongst the goods facilities. All passenger traffic was originally local, but in 1865 the LNWR began services over the newly opened line from Penrith and Keswick. This required a through station at Cockermouth, more centrally placed for the town and sited on the new line before it joined the C&W west of the original terminus, which remained in use for goods until 1964.

In April 1866 the C&W line was joined from the south by the WC&E, which added a new station at Marron Junction and

LNWR engines handled the line's passenger services up to 1923; here a 2-4-0 'Jumbo' hauls a passenger train from Penrith to Whitehaven early in the 20th century. (Railway Photographs, Liverpool)

passenger services from Whitehaven via Moor Row. Later that year the C&W was one of the first lines in West Cumberland to be taken over by the LNWR, which doubled the track and extended Cockermouth's 'new' station with an island platform and a separate refreshment room added in 1890. By 1867 there was a further passenger service, from Maryport to Cockermouth via the Derwent branch to the former C&W line at Brigham (see Chapter 6).

Subsequent through services are covered in the next section, but in terms of local services Cockermouth remained the terminus for trains from Whitehaven and Workington (four to five on weekdays in 1922), as well as those from Whitehaven via Marron Junction, up to the closure of that station and the removal of its east curve. Maryport–Cockermouth services over the Derwent branch lasted until 1935, and local station closures continued with Broughton

The later station at Cockermouth with a crowded platform around 1905. (Author's collection)

Nothing remains of the stations at Cockermouth, but this viaduct (rebuilt in the 1940s) is still in use for a cycleway. (Author)

Cross in 1942, Workington Bridge in 1951, and Camerton the next year. Brigham and Cockermouth survived until the line east to Keswick shut to passenger services on 16th April 1966, the last train being the 8.19 pm DMU from Keswick.

Little of the route survives today. At Workington the trackbed has been landscaped, while a stretch of 2½ miles is used for the A66 road past Brigham and Broughton Cross. The latter's station house survives as a residence, along with later station buildings at Camerton. All five crossings of the Derwent have been demolished, but the bridge over the Marron survives close to the former junction.

Cockermouth–Keswick–Penrith

Although the C&W attempted to extend eastwards in 1846, it was only the development of the West Cumberland iron ore reserves in the next decade that led to a realistic project. The smelting of the ore at that time required higher grade coking coal than could be supplied in West Cumberland, but which was available from County Durham. Thus it was the South Durham & Lancashire Union Railway and Eden Valley Railway that first linked that area to the eastern side of the Lake District at Penrith in 1862 (see Chapter 8). By then the Cockermouth, Keswick & Penrith Railway (CK&P) had been incorporated to build the 30¾ mile line needed to complete the link between West Cumberland and Durham. Passing to the south of the peaks of Skiddaw and Blencathra, and following the River Greta and the shore of Bassenthwaite Lake, the route crossed the Lake District from east to west reaching a summit at 889 ft above sea level near Troutbeck.

The single-track line was engineered by Thomas Bouch, and required the exceptionally high number of 135 bridges, including viaducts at Penruddock and Mosedale (which still survives). It

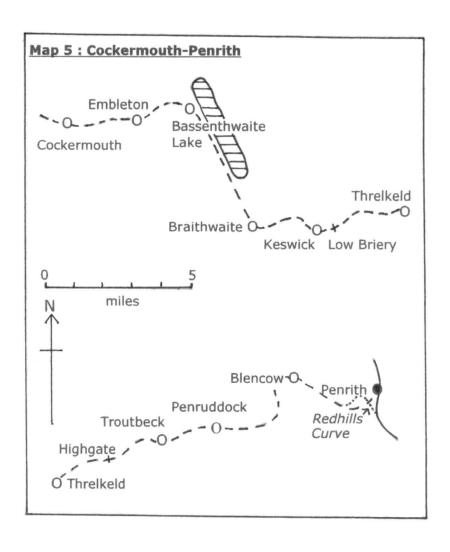

opened for freight in 1864 and to passengers on 2nd January 1865. There was no special opening train, but directors and officials travelled on the first regular train, decorated for the occasion, before adjourning to Keswick's Derwentwater Hotel. Although the CK&P remained independent until 1923, its services were provided by the LNWR, except for mineral shipments to and from County Durham which were handled by the NER. Initially there were three weekday passenger trains each way, rising to seven in the summer of 1900 and eight to nine by 1914. On Sundays, there were never more than one or two trains, and long spells with no trains at all. Stations were built at Embleton, Bassenthwaite Lake, Braithwaite, Keswick (the headquarters of the company with its offices on the upper floor), Threlkeld, Troutbeck, Penruddock and Blencow. There were also halts at Low Briery, east of Keswick, in use for workers at a bobbin mill until closure in 1958, and at Highgate, west of Troutbeck, used by schoolchildren from 1908 to 1928.

Although it was the industries of West Cumberland that prompted the line's development, tourism soon became important. Barely four months after opening, 1,200 day-trippers travelled by train to Keswick on Easter Monday 1865, and the first excursion trip a year later carried 3–4,000 people from Preston on four 'monster' trains for a fare of 3/- each. This led the company to discourage such mass invasions, preferring to maintain Keswick's genteel image. Instrumental in this was the Keswick Hotel, built on land purchased by the railway company and completed in 1869 with 76 guest rooms. Despite this policy the numbers of summer visitors to Keswick by train continued to increase, boosting the line's annual passenger numbers to a peak of over 482,000 in 1913, with through carriages from London, Birmingham, Bletchley, Liverpool, Manchester, Leeds, Bradford, York and Newcastle. To ease the congestion of summer trains, the line was double-tracked from Penrith west to Threlkeld by 1901.

By 1920, the line had entered a long slow decline. Passenger numbers were down to 361,526 that year and the Durham–West Cumberland mineral trade finished by the end of the decade. Long-distance tourist traffic was still important, particularly for the annual evangelical conference known as the Keswick Convention. The 1920s did see the introduction of the most famous summer train to the Lake District though. This started in the summer of 1922 working from London Euston to Windermere, with through coaches for Blackpool, Keswick and Whitehaven. By 1927 it had been named the 'Lakes Express', and six years later its Keswick portion was up to three coaches. After a break for the Second World War (when the Keswick Hotel was used by Roedean School), the 'Lakes Express' was restored and continued to run until 1965.

In January 1955, DMUs were introduced for the Penrith–Keswick–Workington service, leaving the Workington portion of the 'Lakes Express' as the only daily steam working on the line. Blencow station was reopened (it had shut in 1952) and there was a summer weekday service of nine trains each way, including the 'Lakes Express' through carriage for London. There were four extra trains on summer Saturdays, with through carriages for Liverpool, Manchester and Carlisle. However, a survey in 1961 reported that less than 20% of Keswick's visitors were arriving by train and suggested the line was losing £50,000 a year.

The line was recommended for closure in the Beeching Report, and passenger services west of Keswick ended on 16th April 1966. There was strong support for keeping the rest of the line open for Keswick's tourist trade, and its retention had been backed by a TUCC hearing in 1963. The line was singled instead

*A DMU at Threlkeld on the last day of services to Keswick, 4th March 1972.
(Howard S. Morley)*

and its stations reduced to unstaffed halts in 1968. By then there were only six Keswick–Penrith trains daily in summer, with just one extra on Saturdays and no long-distance trains or through carriages. In 1970 a county council survey showed only 1,884 rail journeys in and out of Keswick during a Monday–Saturday period in mid-July (apart from 400 leaving on a Convention special on the Saturday). BR applied for closure again in 1971, claiming that it would cost £117,000 to operate the line in 1972 as against takings of only £14,000 from fares. This time closure was approved, with the last trains running on 4th March 1972. BR had agreed that the final train could be run as a special charter by the Penrith and Keswick Round Tables, and so at 8 pm the 'Farewell Special' with almost 450 passengers was seen off from Keswick by the town band and the 'Miss Cumberland' beauty queen!

Bassenthwaite Lake station had a full range of buildings in 1976, ten years after closure. (Author's collection)

Today, the stationmaster's house is still a residence but this is the former station building in a state of dereliction. (Author)

Keswick station after the line was singled in 1968, but still with its island platform, water tank and signal box. (Author's collection)

Today, only the main building survives, but this has been well restored as part of the adjoining hotel. (J. Suggitt)

*One of the eight bowstring bridges on the railway trail east of Keswick, this
one inverted and clearly showing the massive centre girder added in 1933.
(Author)*

To the west of Keswick, the scenic route along the shore of
Lake Bassenthwaite was used for improvements to the A66
trunk road, the 9¾-mile stretch making it one of the longest rail-
to-road conversions in the country. Only the station buildings
at Bassenthwaite Lake and station houses at Embleton and
Braithwaite remain on this section, while east of Keswick there
are similar survivals at most station sites except Penruddock.
At Keswick the station's island platform and its buildings were
demolished and the site used for a car park, but the restored
main buildings are a reminder of the railway's part in the town's
development, along with the former railway hotel. The station
also marks the start of one of the most spectacular railway
footpaths in the country, the two mile stretch through the Greta
gorge, including eight bowstring girder bridges and a surviving

tunnel. These were purchased with the trackbed between Keswick and Threlkeld by the Lake District National Park authority in 1983. However, there is an active campaign for the return of rail services to Keswick, in the form of the Cockermouth, Keswick & Penrith Reinstatement Group, but in 2008 this remained a project for the future.

6
Solway Plains and Coast

The Mealsgate loop
The Derwent branch
The Port Carlisle branch
The Silloth branch
The Solway Junction Railway

The last railtour over these lines was the 'Solway Ranger' in June 1964, seen here near Drumburgh headed by ex-Great North of Scotland Railway no 49 'Gordon Highlander'. (D. Burdon collection)

The Mealsgate loop

The Maryport & Carlisle (M&C) Railway's Act of 1837 was the first for a line wholly within Cumberland. The resulting 28-mile

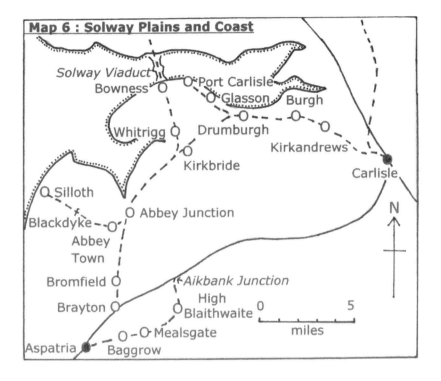

Map 6 : Solway Plains and Coast

railway was built in stages and opened throughout in 1845. The M&C went on to build two more passenger branches to complete a 42¾-mile system, which remained an independent and prosperous concern until the Grouping of 1923 when it became part of the LMS. The first of its offshoots was the Mealsgate loop, also called the Bolton loop from the coalfield it was built to exploit. This was the northern section of the West Cumberland coalfield, extending east along the valley of the River Ellen to Mealsgate, where coal had been mined as early as 1567.

The North British-backed Silloth company put forward proposals in 1861–2 for a branch from Abbey Town to tap this area of the coalfield. To counter this the M&C obtained an Act later in 1862 for what became the Mealsgate loop. The 7¾ mile

One of the last surviving ex-M&C locos, 0-4-2 no 16, seen here as LMS no 10013. (Real Photographs)

'loop' was in fact two branches from the M&C main line, one east from Aspatria and the other west from Aikbank Junction, which met at Mealsgate. They were operated as two separate lines with very little through working, and opened for goods traffic in 1866. The two branches climbed to a summit at over 300 ft above sea level at Mealsgate, with gradients up to 1 in 60 on the eastern section. This gave difficulties for loaded coal trains and the M&C had to replace the tank locos bought for the branch with more powerful tender engines.

A passenger service was introduced on the western section, from Aspatria where a new bay platform was built, to stations at Baggrow and Mealsgate, beginning on Boxing Day 1866. However, the eastern section soon went out of use, with the rails removed from a 1½-mile stretch by 1869. They were replaced by 1872 and passenger services of sorts were introduced over

An early view of Mealsgate station, possibly taken at the track relaying of the 1870s. (Author's collection)

Mealsgate station building is the line's principal surviving remnant. (Author)

the whole loop five years later. On the western section there was a service of five or six weekday Aspatria–Mealsgate trains, known locally as the 'Baggra Bus'. To the east there was only a single 'mixed' train to and from Wigton, which did not connect with any of the Aspatria trains at Mealsgate, but did call at the eastern section's only station at High Blaithwaite. This service was suspended for a coal strike in 1912 and finished completely in 1921. By then the local mines were almost worked out and the western end's passenger trains only lasted for another nine years, although its goods services lingered for a further 22 years before abandonment in 1952. Now all that is left of the line is the former station building at Mealsgate.

The Derwent branch

This 6-mile branch, shown on Map 4, linked the M&C main line at Bullgill to the Workington–Cockermouth line at Brigham. Although shorter than the Mealsgate loop, it had more significance as a through route for both passengers and freight. This stemmed from an agreement made with the LNWR in 1866 whereby half the iron ore sent from the WC&E system to Scotland would use the branch, making it in effect an extension of the Moor Row to Marron Junction line. Later the C&WJ's Northern Extension added traffic from that system, while for fifteen years passengers could travel between Keswick and Carlisle using the branch.

The line was authorised in 1865 and was quickly built, opening to goods traffic in April 1867 and for passengers two months later. Branch platforms were added at Bullgill and Brigham at each end of the line and intermediate stations at Dearham, Dovenby and Papcastle. The latter was at least in later years a 'signal stop', passengers wishing to join the train there had to alert a platelayer's wife living nearby who would set the signal   for

Papcastle station, seen after closure and track-lifting in the 1930s. (Lens of Sutton Association)

The buildings are still recognisable today, despite encroaching vegetation. (Author)

The former private station at Dovenby is also still in use as a residence. (Author)

the train to stop. Dovenby was a private station throughout its existence, built for the sole use of the Dykes family of Dovenby Hall, one of whom was the chairman of the M&C in the 1840s (it is reckoned that the M&C had two of the eight British stations to remain in private ownership). In 1922, the line had five to six weekday passenger trains each way, some linking Maryport and Cockermouth, despite the need for reversals at both Bullgill and Brigham. However, two were Carlisle–Keswick trains, introduced by the M&C in 1920; this service was continued by the LMS with through carriages up to the closure of the branch.

A short-lived addition to the passenger facilities was at Linefoot, where the line from Calva Junction had joined the branch in 1887, but this station was only in use for services on the C&WJ for two months in 1908. The end of through services by that company (along with the closure of the Solway Viaduct) in 1921 marked the end of the line's importance for freight, and it is surprising that the passenger and local goods services lasted until 1935. Once closed on 29th April the line was soon lifted, leading to a tragic accident on 16th December 1936 when the girder bridge over the Derwent near Brigham collapsed during demolition, killing two men. Little is left at the northern end of the branch but further south both Papcastle station buildings and the private station at Dovenby survive, and two remaining piers of the bridge over the Derwent can be seen from the A66.

The Port Carlisle branch

It was a common occurrence for canals to be bought up by railway companies, but rarely was the rail line actually laid in the bed of the canal as happened with this branch. The canal had been opened in 1823, linking Carlisle to the highest navigable point on the Solway Firth which could be reached by ships of up to 100 tons. The canal was mostly for goods, but from 1833 a ferry operated between Port Carlisle and Liverpool, whose passengers included German and Polish emigrants bound for America. These had travelled on the Newcastle & Carlisle Railway, which opened a 1½-mile branch to the canal basin in Carlisle in 1837. Eight years later, the Maryport & Carlisle main line was completed, and Port Carlisle's trade went into decline, leading to the closure of the canal in 1853.

As early as 1847 conversion to a railway had been discussed, and once the canal shut the Port Carlisle Dock & Railway Company was swiftly formed and only ten months later the first passenger train ran on 22nd June 1854, with no opening ceremony at all. 'Scarcely more than a dozen' people travelled on the first train, watched by a few spectators. Over thirty years earlier an estimated crowd of 26,400 had watched the first vessel arrive in

Carlisle's canal basin. The new railway's trains took 35 minutes for the 11 mile journey, starting at a short-lived Canal station at the Carlisle end, followed by Kirkandrews, Burgh (Burgh-by-Sands from 1923), Drumburgh and Glasson (which was always a request stop) before the terminus at Port Carlisle. However, the conversion did not mean the port was any more able to compete with Maryport, Workington and Whitehaven, and its owners were already looking at an alternative site at Silloth. This was to be reached by a new line from Drumburgh, and when this was speedily constructed and opened in 1856, the Drumburgh–Port Carlisle section became a backwater, though with rails instead of its former canal!

The line's reduced status was soon emphasised by the most famous feature of its workings, the 'Dandy' service. This was a passenger coach hauled along the track between Drumburgh and Port Carlisle by a horse, a system that stayed in use for well over fifty years. It was introduced in 1857, although steam engines continued to handle the branch's goods traffic up to 1898. By then the track was in such poor condition that only special freight could be handled, again by horse traction. Four vehicles were used at various times on the passenger service, the most famous being 'Dandy No 1', still in use in 1914 though built in 1861 and now at the National Railway Museum, York. Eventually the NBR, which finally absorbed the branch along with the Silloth line in 1880, decided to replace this anachronism. The first attempt to reintroduce steam traction in 1908 failed due to the poor standard of the track, but heavier rails were laid and six years later England's last horse-hauled passenger service was at last replaced.

The final running of the 'Dandy' was on Saturday 4th April 1914, and two days later NBR class R 0-6-0T no 22 hauled the 'first' steam train of the new era. Crowds of people attended both

The last day of the Port Carlisle 'Dandy' on 4th April 1914. (Carlisle Library)

*Two days later, steam-hauled services returned with North British loco no 22.
(Carlisle Library)*

The station at Kirkandrews, with a seed warehouse in the background. (Author's collection)

The station survives, though much extended, with the remains of the warehouse behind. (Author)

Only the platform is left of the station at Port Carlisle, though the playground indicated by the sign is on the former goods yard. (Author)

events, and so many wanted to travel on the two-coach steam train that extra trips had to be made. During the First World War the service was suspended between January 1917 and February 1919. When it resumed passengers had been lost to the local buses, and despite attempts to attract trippers from Carlisle, the trains were soon cut back to only two weekday return trips from Drumburgh. The LNER made a last try at boosting traffic with Sentinel railcars from Carlisle in 1928, and one of these, *Flower of Yarrow*, was the last passenger working to Port Carlisle on 31st May 1932. Goods services finished on the same day, and the line beyond Drumburgh was abandoned, although the original line from there to Carlisle stayed in use for the Silloth trains for another 32 years. Little can be seen of the line in Carlisle, but its route through Kirkandrews and Burgh is marked by numerous cuttings, many denoting the line of the canal, while

The massive stonework of the former lock entrance at Port Carlisle. (Author)

from Dykesfield to Drumburgh the 2½ mile embankment that carried both canal and railway can be walked. Kirkandrews and Burgh station buildings survive, though much altered, but nothing remains at the sites of Drumburgh and Glasson stations. Only a platform is left at Port Carlisle, and the lock entrance is all that remains of the harbour.

The Silloth branch

Construction of this line began with great ceremony at Drumburgh on 31st August 1855. A gaily decorated engine had driven out from Carlisle, and Sir James Graham cut the first sod as the Warwick Band played *God Save The Queen*. Construction was rapid across the level Solway plain and a year later there was a second ceremony on 28th August 1856, when the company's directors, the Mayor and Corporation of Carlisle, two bands and at least 1,500 passengers travelled on two special trains for the line's opening, which was followed by a dinner for 350 guests in a tent by the newly constructed hotel.

Almost everything at Silloth was 'new' as before the railway came there were only a few hamlets and scattered farms in the area. It had been chosen as the site of the Solway coast's first wet dock in 1852, when the Carlisle & Silloth Bay Dock & Railway Company was formed. In fact the dock was not opened until 1859, by which time the Newcastle & Carlisle had agreed with the NER to route its East–West freight via York and Liverpool rather than Carlisle. Thus much of Silloth's potential trade was lost from the start; instead hopes were pinned on a takeover by the NBR and the development of tourism at Silloth. For this the company had purchased nearly 200 acres of land for a town, where it had built a hotel at a cost of over £7,000, and overseen the construction of public baths, lodging houses, residences, gasworks and a sewerage system, all without any authorisation.

All this left the company on the verge of bankruptcy, and in 1859 it and the Port Carlisle line were leased to the NBR. The latter introduced steamship services to Ireland and Liverpool, and improved the port facilities. Meanwhile the passenger services continued, with four or five daily trains each way, which were only well used in summer. There was little traffic from the intermediate stations at Kirkbride, Abbey (Abbey Town from 1889), Abbeyholme, which became Abbey Junction with the opening of the Solway Junction line to passengers in 1870, and Black Dykes (Blackdyke Halt from 1921).

The NBR tried to develop other traffic, for example building a halt for Silloth Convalescent Home on the Bliterlees branch from the terminus. In 1886 this was extended to the Silloth Battery, built by Armstrong Whitworth for testing heavy guns and in use

Ex-LMS class 4F 0-6-0 no 64478, with a passenger train at Silloth station. (G. Hearse)

until 1926. Passenger specials were run for the visits of military leaders, including at least one Royal Visit. There were many incoming excursions, especially from Carlisle in the summer, and also outgoing ones to agricultural events such as the Westmorland Show at Kendal in 1897 when 34 coaches were needed. Seven years previously, keen to promote its own achievements, the NBR had run five special trains from the branch for the opening of the Forth Railway Bridge.

The line continued to be busy with summer visitors, and freight to and from the port. The remaining passenger sailings to Liverpool, Ireland and the Isle of Man virtually ended during the First World War, and Abbey Junction station closed in 1921. Little changed under the LNER; the line and port were particularly busy during the Second World War. However, after 1945 the line went into decline, with lack of maintenance and loss of freight.

Abbey Town station in 1953, eleven years before closure. (A.G. Ellis collection)

Drumburgh station closed in 1955, but passenger numbers to Silloth could still be significant, with, for example, over 3,000 visitors by rail on Whit Monday 1963.

However, the Beeching Report claimed the line was losing £23,500 a year, and recommended closure. Despite the findings of a TUCC hearing and an 8,000 strong petition, the end for goods services was scheduled for 1st June 1964 and for passenger trains three months later. There was not to be a handful of locals and enthusiasts to see the last train, instead on Saturday 5th September a crowd of over 1,000 people packed the terminus amidst scenes uncommon for a British railway closure. The last day trains were not the usual two-car DMU set, introduced in 1954, but comprised eight coaches, hauled by a diesel loco for the 11.35 am and 6 pm departures from Silloth, but then for the final one, scheduled for 7.58 pm, by class 4 2-6-0 no 43139, known as *Jezebel* at Carlisle's Kingsmoor shed. This train was at first unable

By June 2007 the former station buildings at Silloth were a pile of rubble, but the platform and gable-fronted station house (right background) survived. (Author)

Unlike Port Carlisle, Silloth still retains its port facilities including the New Dock opened by the NBR in 1885. (Author)

to reach the platform at Silloth due to demonstrators sitting on the track. When these were moved, and four extra coaches added for the return journey, the same happened again until the line was cleared by railway police. Even then there was a further delay for a bomb hoax before the train reached Carlisle where the passengers were herded away by police for fear of further trouble.

After such a dramatic finale, the track was speedily removed and now there is little left, although Kirkbride, Abbey Town and Black Dykes station houses remain as residences. Silloth station building, though much altered, survived until 2007 and was then demolished, though the port and seaside resort are still there as reminders of a failed railway enterprise.

The Solway Junction Railway

This line crossing the Solway Firth must surely have been the most extraordinary and least used of all the cross-Border rail routes between England and Scotland. As with so many Cumbrian railways, mineral traffic was the reason for the project. The promoters of the Dumfriesshire and Cumberland (Solway Junction) Railway in 1862 saw the line as a shortcut for Cumberland iron ore to reach the furnaces of Lanarkshire. A 20-mile line would link Kirtlebridge on the Caledonian in Scotland to the M&C station at Brayton. This had been built in 1845 as another of the M&C's 'private' stations for Sir Wilfrid Lawson, who agreed three years later to its use by the public! Complex negotiations led to the English section joining the Silloth line near Abbey Town and leaving it at Kirkbride Junction, reducing the Solway Junction Railway (as incorporated in 1864) to 17¼ miles of track. Work began on its 1,950 yds long viaduct of 193 spans in March 1865, using barges to carry the girders out to a stage in the middle of the Firth. When finished in 1868 it was the longest railway viaduct in the world and was reported to have cost £100,000. However, the line's completion was further delayed by difficulties in crossing Bowness Moss south of the viaduct, where the peat was 50 ft deep in places. Goods traffic began in September 1869 without any ceremony, but the Board of Trade refused to allow passenger traffic south of Bowness until the route across the moss was further consolidated. Eventually the first passenger train over the whole route, an excursion from Aspatria to Dumfries, ran on 28th July 1870.

Regular passenger services between Brayton and Kirtlebridge began in August 1870, with three trains each way on weekdays, worked by the Caledonian. These called at stations provided at Abbey Junction, Whitrigg, and Bowness on the English side, and Annan (Annan Shawhill from 1924) in Scotland. An additional English station was opened at Broomfield (Bromfield from 1895)

The Solway Junction Railway had its own engines, although operated by the Caledonian Railway. This is 0-6-0 no 6, which survived as LMS no 17102 until 1928. (Author's collection)

Brayton, once a private station, was the terminus for Caledonian services over the line in the early 20th century. (Author's collection)

in 1873. The Annan–Kirtlebridge section was transferred to the Caledonian in that year, but the Solway Junction Railway continued to run the rest of the line. It was soon in financial difficulties as the iron ore trade dwindled away, with total revenue declining from £2,038 in 1874 to a loss of £574 six years later. However, it was conditions on the Solway Firth that were to deal the most severe blow to the line's prospects. The estuary had always been regarded as one of the most treacherous in Britain, with scouring tides racing at up to twelve knots, and the viaduct was damaged by frost and gales on thirty occasions. Conditions were at their worst in the winter of 1880–1, referred to as a 'great freeze', when the rivers Eden and Esk flowing into the Firth froze solid. When these began to thaw in January 1881, 'icebergs' as large as 27 yds square and 6 ft thick were reported in the Solway.

The Solway Viaduct seen from the English shore around 1910. (Carlisle Library)

All that remains on the English side of the viaduct are these rusting piers at the end of the 460 yds long, stone-faced embankment. (Author)

This isolated building is all that remains of the former station at Abbey Junction. (Author)

The railway's response was to put an overnight watch of four men in a cabin on the viaduct. In the early morning of Sunday 30th January the force of the ice was so great that the four had to abandon their cabin and get ashore. By the following Wednesday, 45 piers of the 193 had collapsed leaving two gaps, one of 900 ft.

Surprisingly considering its finances, the company set about repairing and strengthening the viaduct. By May 1884 it was back in use with five passenger trains each way on weekdays. In 1895 the line was absorbed by the Caledonian, which ran down the already limited passenger service to three weekday trains by 1908 and a single passenger coach attached to goods trains in the First World War, when the intermediate stations closed for over two years. They reopened with a single mixed train each way in 1919, but two years later the Caledonian was faced with the need for £70,000 worth of repairs to the viaduct and closed it instead.

There were another ten years of passenger services on the Scottish side, but in England only the Brayton–Abbey Junction section saw goods trains and occasional excursions until final closure in 1933. Meanwhile, the viaduct had continued to be used as an unofficial walkway, particularly by Scots crossing for the less restrictive Sunday licensing laws in England, despite the dangers of the return journey over the decaying structure. Demolition began in 1934, lasting nineteen months and costing the lives of three workers swept away and drowned in the current. Even after its removal the viaduct caused problems as the stones sunk to protect it had created a reef. Gangs of workmen from the railway worked intermittently for years breaking and scattering the stones before the Firth was made safe for shipping. Today nothing can be seen except rusting piers at the end of the embankment near Bowness, where the station house is now a residence. The former station building at Abbey Junction also survives, but the route across the flat Solway plains has almost disappeared.

7
Main Line into Scotland: The Waverley Route in Cumbria

North British memories; restored 4-4-0 no 256 'Glen Douglas', one of the company's class K locos that still worked the Waverley Route in the early 1960s, on a railtour at Langholm. (J. Davenport)

The former North British Railway's Carlisle–Edinburgh line, referred to as the Waverley Route as early as 1862, is with some justification usually thought of as a Scottish line. The bulk of its 98¼ mile length, its principal intermediate stations, the outcry against closure and the proposed reinstatement of some of its

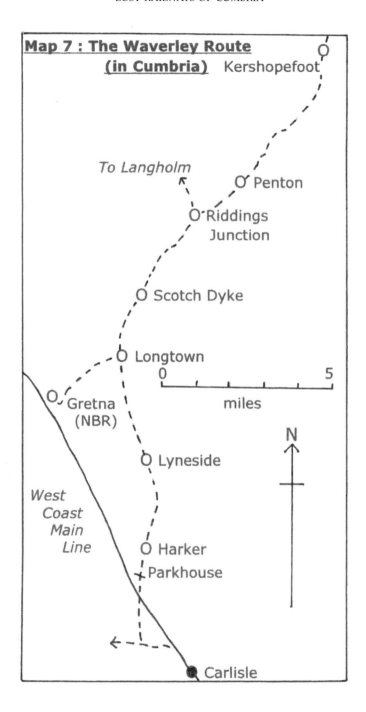

Map 7 : The Waverley Route
(in Cumbria) Kershopefoot

To Langholm

Penton

Riddings
Junction

Scotch Dyke

Longtown

0   5

Gretna
(NBR)

miles

N

Lyneside

West
Coast
Main
Line

Harker

Parkhouse

Carlisle

services, all lie within Scotland. Nevertheless the 21¼ miles of former trackbed, nine stations and halts (in use at various times) and the start of two branches are a significant part of Cumbria's lost railways and so will be dealt with here. The North British Railway (NBR) was incorporated in 1844 and while its early major concern was the Edinburgh-Berwick line, within a year it had begun what was to become the Waverley Route, by the purchase in 1845 of the Edinburgh & Dalkeith Railway, with powers to extend to Hawick. Four years later this branch, originally a horse-worked line of 4 ft 6 inch gauge but now standard gauge and steam-worked, was part of the NBR's Edinburgh–Hawick line. The battle to build a Hawick–Carlisle link lasted the next ten years as the NBR and its bitter rival the Caledonian Railway fought to get rival routes through Parliament. Eventually in 1859 a nominal subsidiary – the Border Union Railway – was empowered to build the NBR's line into England, using what has been described as a 'desperately bad choice of route' in climbing to a summit at 900 ft above sea level and including a 20-mile stretch almost devoid of settlement.

Southbound the route crossed the Border close to the first of its English stations at Kershopefoot. It then followed the valley of the Liddel Water, which here marks the Border, but always keeping to the English side, through a short-lived station at Nook Pasture, and one at Penton, to Riddings Junction, the station for the 7-mile long Langholm branch. Another minor station at Scotch Dyke followed, then the only sizeable settlement on the English section at Longtown, which was also the start of the NBR branch to Gretna. The route of the main line from here to Carlisle was affected by the NBR's battle with the Caledonian. Originally the plan was for the two companies' lines to join at Rockcliffe, but due to the

Kershopefoot was the line's northernmost station within England.
(Author's collection)

Caledonian's opposition, the NBR took a more easterly course
from Longtown through minor stations at Lyneside (originally
West Linton, then briefly Lineside) and Harker, and a much
later halt at Parkhouse, to reach the Port Carlisle line, whose
link to the Caledonian had already been authorised in 1858. By
negotiating a lease (along with the Silloth line) the NBR gained
access into Carlisle's Citadel station. However, its use of 1¼
miles of Caledonian track led to wrangles, arbitration and a
delayed start to passenger services. Strangely for a Scottish
company, these began from the Carlisle end, as far as Scotch
Dyke on 29th October 1861. The following March these were
extended into Scotland but it was 1st July before a Carlisle–
Edinburgh service began.

It was another 14 years before the line achieved national
significance. In 1876 the Midland Railway completed its Settle &

The line in use: ex-LNER class V2 2-6-2 no 60934 with an Edinburgh–London King's Cross passenger train near the Scottish border in 1952. (E.R. Morten)

The line abandoned: Stow station over the border in Scotland in 1972, three years after the line closed. (Author's collection)

Carlisle line, providing a through route from London St Pancras. An agreement was reached whereby the NBR would work the Midland's Scotch Express trains, including Britain's first Pullman cars, north from Carlisle, an arrangement that continued up to the Grouping. It was a NBR class M 4-4-0 engine that achieved a record time of 2 hours 6 minutes for the demanding Carlisle–Edinburgh run in the Railway Races of 1901, as compared with over 4½ hours for the 'parliamentary' train stopping at all stations. However, the line was woefully underused; in 1922, just before the Grouping there were only five expresses and two stopping trains on weekdays between Carlisle and Hawick (plus two Carlisle–Langholm stopping trains) and a solitary Sunday express. The next year the line became part of the LNER, but in 1927 it was the LMS that began the line's most famous working – the London St Pancras–Edinburgh 'Thames-Forth Express', renamed the 'Waverley' in 1957. To cope with such services on their Carlisle–Edinburgh section, in 1929 the LNER brought in its Gresley-designed Pacific locos., such as the Class A3 4-6-2. These, including some based at Carlisle Canal shed, continued in use on the line until the 1960s, although dieselisation of most services early in the decade meant the end of Carlisle-based traction on these long-distance trains.

However, it was the line's local services that were the first to go. The branch to Gretna lost its meagre passenger service of two trains on weekdays in 1915, when the line was requisitioned by the War Office. Lyneside and Harker stations shut in 1929 (although the latter had a limited reopening in 1936–41) and Scotch Dyke in 1949. Riddings Junction closed when the Langholm branch service of five to six trains on weekdays was withdrawn in 1964, leaving only Longtown, Penton and Kershopefoot of the English stations still in use by local passenger trains. Closure of the whole line was formally proposed in 1966, when it was seen as duplicating

Lyneside was an early station closure in 1929. (Author's collection)

The station at Lyneside is still recognisable today with even the lower part of the former signal box still in use. (Author)

The NBR's route into Carlisle is still marked by this fine viaduct over the River Eden. (Author)

other Anglo-Scottish passenger routes, despite its usefulness when either the East or West Coast routes were blocked. Even by 1949 its main use had been for goods, with fourteen express freights and two pick-up goods trains daily compared with the remaining four passenger expresses and three stopping trains covering the whole stretch from Hawick south to Carlisle. Only weeks before the Beeching Report recommended closure, BR had opened links for freight trains from the Waverley Route into the newly opened Kingmoor yard near Carlisle. Although attempts were made to save the route north of Hawick, the section within England attracted few supporters. Not that it made much difference, as the whole line closed amidst much protest on the night of 5th/6th January 1969.

A lost trunk line; all that is left of the Waverley Route south of Lyneside. (Author)

While 40 years later the Scottish section of the line has preservation groups active at Riccarton Junction and Whitrope, plus plans well under way to restore the Edinburgh–Hawick service, the English stretch has almost disappeared. It is even said that the M6 north of Carlisle was built across its route on the level to forestall any attempt at reopening. At almost no point is the trackbed officially walkable, and the only remaining buildings are the former station house at Lyneside, and the buildings at Penton and Scotch Dyke station, where a restored canopy caption still reads 'Speed and comfort by rail'! A viaduct over the Esk also survives at Scotch Dyke, along with one crossing the Liddel Water (and the Border) on the Langholm branch close to the former Riddings Junction, and one over the Eden at Carlisle. However it is the little-known Gretna branch that has survived best, with its station building intact over 90 years after closure, and 1¾ miles still with track leading into a military depot.

8
Eastern Fringes

The Brampton branch
The South Tynedale Railway
The Stainmore Route
The Eden Valley line
Low Gill–Ingleton–Clapham

On the eastern boundary: 2-6-0 no 43102, built by BR to Ivatt's last design for the LMS, heads past the cottages near Stainmore summit with a Blackpool –Darlington train. (C. Ord collection)

The Brampton branch

Situated in the far north-east of Cumbria, this very short line of 1¼ miles was the passenger-carrying section of a much longer freight system that extended high onto the fells and over to Lambley on the Alston branch. Often referred to as Lord Carlisle's Railway after the local landowner (and owner of the railway up to 1911), this began as one of the country's earliest wooden wagon-ways, opened in 1799 for horse-drawn shipments of coal and lime to a depot at the small town of Brampton. Ten years later it was relaid, with both cast iron and wrought iron rails, the country's first such commercially successful use of the latter. It was also now at a gauge of 4 ft 8½ inches, possibly the first use outside George Stephenson's railways, and by 1833 was being used by horse-drawn 'Dandy' carriages for passengers. During 1834–6 the wagon-way was replaced at the Brampton end by 3½ miles of railway on a new route further south. This line became the first in Cumberland to have steam-hauled passenger trains when on 15th July 1836, two engines, *Atlas* and *Gilsland*, were hired for the official opening ceremony.

Later in 1836 the line became home to one of the most celebrated engines of all time when Stephenson's *Rocket* was purchased from the Liverpool & Manchester Railway for £300. This was for the freight traffic, but by 1840 it had proved too light and was replaced by two engines built at the line's own works at Kirkhouse. Meanwhile the 'Dandy' carriages continued in use for passengers, with services between a coal staith at Brampton and the station at Milton (renamed Brampton Junction in 1870) on the Carlisle–Newcastle line. It is often claimed that once the horse was removed for the final downhill stretch to Brampton, the carriage was only halted by a mound of earth! It seems more likely that this was a gentle descent controlled by the brakesman, although still alarming for many people.

In the 1870s the townspeople of Brampton demanded a 'proper' service, and in 1881 the line was relaid with steel rails, and a small platform plus shelter provided for the town. A

The opening ceremony for Brampton Town station in 1913. (Carlisle Library)

single engine *Dandie Dinmont* was purchased, which with three secondhand four-wheeled carriages handled the passenger service for the next nine years. These passed without incident, remarkably so considering the line failed a Board of Trade inspection in 1890 and the passenger service was withdrawn. Despite lengthy protests, the town was left without passenger trains until 1913. After eight years of negotiations, a 50-year lease of the branch into the town was agreed with the NER, which relaid the line yet again and with much 'pomp and ceremony' reintroduced the passenger service on 31st March 1913.

However, there were not to be anything like 50 years of services. After a promising start with an influx of wartime workers to Brampton, passenger trains were suspended as an economy measure between 1917 and 1920. When they resumed, traffic was by then so light that by 1921 the NER was claiming an annual loss of £3,000. In 1923 the newly-formed LNER was never

An early 20th-century view of Brampton Junction station, with the branch platform behind the fence and nameboard at the left. (Author's collection)

The trackbed of the Brampton branch can still be seen behind a platform at the former Junction station. (Author)

likely to maintain such an unprofitable service, and it ended on 29th October. Even the goods service lasted only two more months, and the line into Brampton Town was lifted in 1924. The rest of the system stayed in use for freight, chiefly coal traffic, for almost another thirty years until closed by the National Coal Board in 1953. The former passenger-carrying section was kept as a path to Brampton Junction station, and is now the 'Dandy Line' footpath allowing walkers to follow the route of the horse, the *Dandie Dinmont*, and the *Rocket*, which of course can still be seen restored as an exhibit at the Science Museum in London.

The South Tynedale Railway

Although almost all the 13-mile Haltwhistle–Alston branch was within Northumberland, the section reopened as the South Tynedale Railway is based at the Cumbrian market town of

LNER days with class G5 0-4-4T no 7315 at Alston station in the late 1940s. (Author's collection)

The preservation scene, with Hunslet diesel 0-4-0 no 9 on passenger service. (Author)

Alston. The original branch opened throughout in 1852, but lost its goods services in 1965, with the last passenger trains on 1st May 1976. Consent for the final closure had been given by the Department of the Environment as early as January 1973, and three months later the South Tynedale Railway Preservation Society was formed. Although the intention was to save the whole branch, this proved impossible to achieve and BR began lifting the track later in 1976. Even the cost of a more modest scheme to save the final 1½ miles to Alston could not be met, so in June 1977 the Society decided to concentrate instead on a narrow gauge scheme for the line.

Negotiations began with Cumbria and Northumberland County Councils who had the first option to buy the trackbed. The Alston end became available first, after the Cumbria County

The fine station frontage at Alston has been retained by the preservation society. (Author)

Council decided to acquire the Alston station site and 1½ miles of trackbed in 1977, with agreement to lease the trackbed to the Society reached in June 1980. That year track-laying of the 2 ft gauge line began and the Society acquired its first locomotive. Major repairs to the viaduct over the River South Tyne delayed the opening until 30th July 1983, when at 10.15 am services began on just over a mile of track from Alston, with nearly 5,000 people travelling on the 'new' line in its first short season. The following year over 10,000 passengers were recorded. In 1986 it was extended to a halt at Gilderdale close to the county boundary, with passenger numbers rising to 26,000 by 1992. Progress on the Northumbrian section was slower; although planning permission and access between Gilderdale and Slaggyford were obtained in 1986, a Light Railway Order for this section was not granted for another ten years. Eventually in September 1999 another ¾ mile of the line was

Gala weekend in 2007, with the society's 0-4-0T 'Helen Kathryn' and visiting 0-4-2T 'Stanhope'. (Author)

opened to a 'new' station at Kirkhaugh. In 2007 the trackbed north from there could be walked as part of the South Tyne Trail, which also runs alongside the current narrow gauge railway.

In 2007 the Society operated four or five trains a day at weekends from Easter to October, with daily workings mid-July to the end of August as well as at Easter and Spring Bank Holiday. 'Santa Specials' were run on December weekends and the highlight of the year was the 'Gala Weekend' in September, with all three of the line's steam locomotives in action. These were 0-4-0T *Thomas Edmondson*, built in Germany in 1918, 0-6-0T (and tender) *Naklo*, formerly at work in Polish sugar mills, and *Helen Kathryn*, a later (1948) German-built 0-4-0T. British 2 ft gauge was represented by visiting 0-4-2T *Stanhope*, built by Kerr Stuart in 1917.

'Northern England's highest narrow gauge railway' continues to be a popular visitor attraction, and will be boosted further by the proposed extension to Slaggyford, which unlike Kirkhaugh was a former station on the standard gauge branch and has road access. By the end of 2007 all necessary legal permissions had been obtained for this additional 2½ miles, and work was expected to start on the first half of this in 2008. Such expansion will help boost the line's growing importance amongst the narrow gauge railway preservation schemes in Britain.

The Stainmore Route

The 34¾-mile line between Barnard Castle and Tebay was one of the most challenging to build and work in the country, requiring nine major viaducts and a climb to a summit at 1,370 ft, the second highest used by passenger trains in England. Only the section west of the summit was within Cumbria, but this contained the bulk of the mileage, stations and viaducts. Schemes to cross this area of the Pennines were first put forward in the 'Railway Mania' of 1845/6, but it was the formation of the South Durham & Lancashire Union Railway (SD&LUR) that led to the line being built between 1857 and 1861. By then the aim was not so much to fill a gap in the 'railway map' as to get Durham coke to the developing iron-making industries of Furness and West Cumberland.

The SD&LUR was backed by the Stockton & Darlington Railway (S&D), which had opened the world's first steam-operated railway in 1825. This was extended to Barnard Castle in July 1856, and the SD&LUR was to continue the line westwards over Stainmore to Tebay on the West Coast Main Line. Progress was rapid; the Royal Assent was granted on 13th July 1857, and six weeks later the first sod was cut by the Duke of Cleveland at Kirkby Stephen. Despite the difficult terrain the line was completed within four years and the first mineral trains ran in

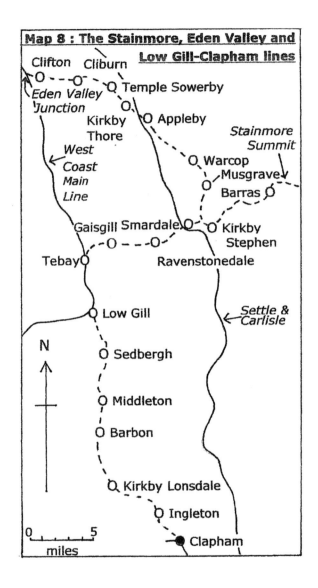

Map 8 : The Stainmore, Eden Valley and Low Gill-Clapham lines

Darlington-based Ivatt 2-6-0 no 43129 heads through the cutting at Bleathgill, a notorious spot for winter snow drifts. (Author's collection)

July 1861. The formal opening was not until 7th August, with public services of two passenger trains each way from the next day. Significantly there were already four mineral trains a day, plus two combined trains for both minerals and goods. All these services were handled by the S&D which absorbed the SD&LUR in 1862, only to become part of the NER the next year.

From the summit the Cumbrian section of the line descended 730 ft over nine miles, at gradients of 1 in 59 to 1 in 72, to just west of Kirkby Stephen. The steepest stretch came first and included the six-span Mousegill Viaduct, ending at Barras, one of the highest main line stations in England. A mile to the south was the line's engineering masterpiece – Belah Viaduct, designed by Thomas Bouch and comprising a 1,040 ft long iron trestle, with 15 piers soaring to 196 ft above the river, making it the highest viaduct in England. Three stone viaducts – Aitygill,

Winter on Stainmore as BR class 4MT no 76052 heads a westbound mineral train past the summit signal box. (P. Wilson)

Merrygill and Podgill, with a total of 29 spans – were crossed before Kirkby Stephen. These three were only built to carry a single track, and additional viaducts had to be built alongside each of them before the doubling of the Barnard Castle–Kirkby Stephen line was completed in the early 1900s. West of Kirkby Stephen there was a 5-mile climb with gradients as steep as 1 in 76 to a second summit at Sandy Bank (889 ft) before a long gradual descent to Tebay. Only one viaduct was required on this stretch, the fourteen-span Smardale Gill Viaduct, and three stations were provided at Smardale, Ravenstonedale and Gaisgill.

By 1900 there were four summer weekday passenger trains between Darlington and Tebay, with four goods trains and thirteen to fifteen mineral trains, mostly from West Auckland. The latter were split at Stainmore for the descent and so there were as many as 30 mineral trains daily west into Kirkby Stephen. Long-distance passenger traffic started in summer 1905, when the Newcastle–Barrow (Ramsden Dock) service began. The next year an extra train from Darlington conveyed through coaches (bound for Keswick) from York and Newcastle as far as Kirkby Stephen. The Newcastle–Barrow service ended in 1911 and, after the Grouping, the long-distance services did not resume until 1932 when both Newcastle–Blackpool trains and the special service from Durham to Ulverston ran during the summer. After a break for the Second World War, the summer holiday trains over Stainmore did not restart until 1949, when a West Hartlepool–Blackpool service was introduced, with from 1953 a summer Saturday Newcastle–Blackpool train as well. By then the local services on the Tebay–Kirkby Stephen section had ended, on 1st December 1952, with the closure of Gaisgill, Smardale and

A view of Ravenstonedale station around 1920 with a NER train. (Author's collection)

135

A snowy scene as Ivatt class 2MT 2-6-0 no 46471 heads a short goods train out of the sidings at Kirkby Stephen East. (A. Ramsay collection)

Ravenstonedale stations, although the latter retained its goods services for another ten years.

The summer workings were then the only passenger trains west of Kirkby Stephen, but a year-round weekday service of three trains each way continued over Stainmore to and from the Eden Valley line. In 1958 this was taken over by DMUs, which improved passenger takings by £1,400, but closure was first proposed the following year. Although freight movements were still substantial, BR claimed that these could be re-routed by the Newcastle–Carlisle line, and that over £100,000 a year would be saved by closing the Stainmore route. Although this figure was later scaled down to £36,000, and in spite of vigorous protests from MPs, councils and industries, closure was eventually approved in December 1961. BR acted quickly on this decision, and the last passenger train ran on 20th January 1962. Normally this would

Tebay station at the western end of the line, with a 1955 railtour headed by ex-LNER class J21 0-6-0 no 65061 about to set off over the route. (A. Chambers)

have been the 8.30 pm diesel from Penrith to Darlington, but this was followed by a steam-hauled excursion on the last leg of its tour from Darlington, with 200 enthusiasts each paying £1.10s for the 200-mile trip. Only a 2-mile stretch around Kirkby Stephen was retained for access to Hartley Quarry, and track-lifting of the remainder began in 1962. Belah and Mousegill viaducts were demolished in 1963 and 1966 respectively, and the final quarry rail traffic in 1974 brought to an end the last use of any part of the Stainmore Route.

Most of the western end of the Stainmore Route can be seen without leaving a car as over five miles of its former trackbed east of Tebay have been used for the A685, ending with a good view of the station buildings at Ravenstonedale. The former line can also be glimpsed from the A66 sweeping east up to Stainmore Summit, where part of its trackbed has been used for road improvements.

Belah, the most famous of the line's viaducts, with BR class 4MT 2-6-0 no 76045 leading a double-headed passenger train. (Author's collection)

Now only the abutments (and a few pier bases) remain at either side of the Belah valley. (Author)

The former station house at Barras in August 2007; the bricks were from the eastbound platform waiting room taken down ready for restoration at the Kirkby Stephen East site. (Author)

East and west from the summit a couple of miles of trackbed within Cumbria are walkable across 'Open Access Land'. Further west both abutments at the site of Belah Viaduct can be accessed by public footpath, but there is nothing left of Mousegill Viaduct, and Aitygill Viaduct is inaccessible. The trackbed west of Rookby Scarth is a concessionary footpath, rather overgrown in places, but from the lane at Hartley a mile of good footpath (easily reached from Kirkby Stephen) leads over the restored Merrygill and Podgill viaducts. Further west, a path through a nature reserve uses over 2½ miles of trackbed between the site of Smardale station and Newbiggin-on-Lune. This passes under the Settle & Carlisle line's Smardale Viaduct, which is still in use, and crosses the restored Smardale Gill Viaduct on the former line to Tebay.

Merrygill is the easternmost of the three stone viaducts near Kirkby Stephen restored by the Northern Viaducts Trust. (Author)

The Eden Valley line

The small town of Kirkby Stephen appears a surprising location for a railway centre of some importance. Well to the south is the former Midland station on the Settle & Carlisle line, still operational today, while nearer the town was the NER station, officially named Kirkby Stephen East in 1950. This originally had twin train sheds, extending over up and down platforms, with offices and waiting rooms between them, and a tower over a lift worked by a turbo-generator driven by the River Eden. There were separate up and down lines for mineral traffic and a complex of sidings for the goods yard. Nearby was an engine shed, originally built for two engines, but as late as 1956 home to fourteen locos, all less than ten years old. The shed closed in its centenary year, 1961, and passenger services ended the next

A close-up view of J21 no 65061 (with class 2MT no 46478) on the 1955 'Northern Dales' rail tour at Kirkby Stephen East station. (Author's collection)

Today, the surviving train shed at Kirkby Stephen East is the home of the Stainmore Railway preservation group. (Author)

Warcop station in the early years of the 20th century. (Author's collection)

year. In 1969 the remains of the station were converted into a bobbin mill which stayed in business until 1992. After a spell of dereliction, the building is now leased to the Stainmore Railway preservation group, and can be visited at weekends.

The Eden Valley line branched off northwards just west of Kirkby Stephen station. This 22-mile single-track line was built by a nominally separate company, the Eden Valley Railway, although four of its directors were shared with the SD&LUR and it too was backed by the S&D. Work began in 1858 and was completed within four years, as construction was easy along the Eden Valley, although three small viaducts were needed. Stations were built at Musgrave, Warcop, Appleby (Appleby East from 1952), Kirkby Thore, Temple Sowerby, and Cliburn, before the line reached the Lancaster & Carlisle line at the latter's Clifton station. The connection here faced south, away from Penrith, and within a year a short branch was built to the north-facing Eden Valley Junction on the main line a mile to the north.

The earlier connection was removed in 1875, while an extra Clifton station was built on the new section, renamed Clifton Moor in 1927; this was notable for its private waiting room built for Lord Lonsdale. The original plan for a separate line into Penrith had been dropped in favour of running powers on the main line, but when the NER absorbed the Eden Valley line in 1863, it applied to build a connection to the CK&P bypassing Penrith. This was the Redhills Curve (shown on Map 5), much used by NER coke trains heading for West Cumberland; it was separate from the Eden Valley line, as it connected two LNWR lines by the time of its opening in 1866. Use of the curve ended with the decline of the coke traffic in the 1920s, although it was not finally closed until 1938. A final short connection was built at

A view showing the fine architectural style of Appleby East station, taken after the line was reduced to single-track for quarry workings in the 1960s.

Appleby to link with the Midland's Settle & Carlisle line, opened after that line's completion in 1876.

Passenger services began in 1862, with the NER mostly concentrating on a branch-line service to and from Kirkby Stephen in connection with the Stainmore trains. In 1922 only one of the line's five weekday trains from Penrith continued on to Darlington. Between 1880 and 1893 there were also two to three NER trains a day between the Midland station at Appleby and Penrith, and in the 1900s through coaches for Keswick from York, Newcastle (and possibly London King's Cross) via Stainmore. The LNER switched most Stainmore services to Penrith rather than Tebay, a precursor of the end of trains to the latter in 1952. There were still three Darlington–Penrith weekday trains each way in the summer of 1955, with one on Sundays (starting from Saltburn). By then the intermediate stations were closing; Musgrave in 1952, Kirkby Thore and Temple Sowerby the next year and Cliburn in 1956. All passenger services ended with the closure of the Stainmore route in January 1962.

The northern half of the line was soon removed, but the spur from the Settle & Carlisle at Appleby was used to give access south to Kirkby Stephen and Hartley Quarry. When the movement of stone by rail ended in 1974, this southern section was cut back to serve the army training camp near Warcop. When this use also finished in 1989, the remaining six miles south of Appleby became derelict, but in 1995 the Eden Valley Railway Society was set up to restore this section. Based at Warcop, the society resumed passenger operations in 2006, using an ex-Southern electric unit over a short stretch of track, but unfortunately in May 2007 a bridge near Warcop was damaged by an army truck and no passenger services were possible that year. Apart from its six miles still with track, the route has retained many of its structures. Although two of its three viaducts were demolished, its former stations are substantially intact, with only Kirkby Thore lost to road improvements. All the other station sites retain at least some buildings, mostly used as residences, with signal boxes surviving at Warcop and Cliburn.

Low Gill–Ingleton–Clapham

In 1846 the 'Little' North Western Railway Company (so called to distinguish it from the LNWR) was incorporated to build lines from Skipton to the Lancaster & Carlisle Railway (L&C), linking the Yorkshire industrial towns with the future main line to Scotland. The scheme included plans for a branch reaching the L&C near Low Gill, but rising construction costs meant that all that was built of this was a 4¼-mile line from Clapham (North Yorks) to Ingleton, opened in 1849. However when the 'Little' North Western completed its Clapham-Lancaster line the following year, the branch to Ingleton closed to passengers after only ten months of operations!

In 1857, after the 'Little' North Western had failed to complete the branch north to Low Gill, the L&C obtained an Act for its own 18¾-mile Ingleton–Low Gill line. By the time this opened without official ceremony in 1861, the L&C had been leased to the LNWR and the 'Little' North Western to the Midland, so it was these two major companies that then met at Ingleton. They were at that time bitter enemies and so the LNWR built its own Ingleton station (and engine shed), with passengers at first forced to walk between the two stations. Although this problem was soon resolved, relations between the two companies remained so bad that the Midland felt compelled to build its own route to Scotland, completing the famous Settle & Carlisle line in 1876.

The line's northern end was at Low Gill station, on the West Coast Main Line, seen here in 1954, the year the branch to Ingleton and Clapham closed to regular passenger services. (Author's collection)

In these circumstances, it is not surprising that the Low Gill–Clapham line never achieved its potential as a through route, although by following the Lune valley it provided a much easier route than the Settle & Carlisle. No tunnels were required but bridges and viaducts were numerous. Major viaducts were required at Ingleton, over the Rawthey near Sedbergh, across the Lune at Waterside, and at Low Gill. Passenger services were sparse: as late as 1922 the LNWR was only providing a basic Tebay–Low Gill–Ingleton service of four weekday trains each way, calling at Sedbergh, Middleton, Barbon, Kirkby Lonsdale and the Midland station at Ingleton, where the LNWR station, known locally as Thornton, had closed in 1917. The Midland's

Ingleton's former Midland station after closure to passengers in 1954, but before demolition. (Author's collection)

Ingleton–Clapham service was a little better at eight weekday trains each way. There were a few long-distance workings, notably a Leeds–Keswick service from 1910 to 1914; this was reintroduced after the Grouping and continued on summer Saturdays up to 1939. Despite these, it was only the Clapham–Ingleton section that saw much traffic, with stone traffic from local quarries and excursions from Leeds and Bradford, as well as the scheduled passenger workings.

Jack Dawson, whose family have operated a coal merchant's business at the former Sedbergh station since 1895, remembered the line as far back as the 1920s. His first memory was of visiting the yard with his father and seeing the morning goods train from Low Gill with a 0-6-0 locomotive. At that time everything in the district came and went by rail, and the yard could be busy with as many as twenty horse-drawn carts. Even in the early

A view of Low Gill Viaduct not seen by motorists on the M6. (Author)

Walkers on the Dales Way pass under the arches of the Lune Viaduct near Sedbergh. (Author)

1950s he remembered morning and afternoon goods trains each weekday, and three deliveries of coal totalling 80–90 tons a week at Sedbergh in winter. There was also some through freight, notably the 'Bamber Bridge Goods' en route for Carlisle, usually hauled by a a 'Black Five' locomotive. Local passenger services were four weekday trains each way, often with only a handful of passengers. Even after these ended there were occasional specials such as ex-LNER no 4472 *Flying Scotsman* in 1963, and diversions, particularly earlier that year when the Settle & Carlisle line was blocked by snow for several weeks.

Middleton, which added '-on-Lune' in 1926, was an early closure five years later, but the remaining stations lasted until the end of passenger services in 1954, with the last trains on Saturday, 30th January. There was much more of a ceremony for

Kirkby Lonsdale station building has been well restored and is now a pottery and arts and crafts centre. (Author)

these than for the opening almost a century earlier, especially for the last train of all which departed at 6.42 pm from Clapham. Five coaches were packed for the occasion, with many people in Victorian costume, and the Kirkby Lonsdale brass band whose predecessors had performed on the line's opening day. At Low Gill there were speeches and a wreath laid on the loco, and back at Ingleton a final rendition of *Auld Lang Syne*!

Trains for the boarding schools in the Lune valley continued to run at the beginning and end of terms, but the goods workings had been reduced to three a week from 1956 and the line was being maintained to main line standards for such limited use. This ended in 1964 when freight was cut back to Clapham–Ingleton and the schools service was discontinued. The line was finally closed the next year, with the track lifted in 1967.

The route is now notable for its viaducts, as all the major examples survive. Ingleton's is easily seen from the village, and the Rawthey and Lune viaducts can be approached on foot, but the one most often seen is the graceful curve of eleven stone arches at Low Gill, glimpsed by motorists speeding by on the nearby M6 motorway. Little of the line can be walked, but station buildings survive at Kirkby Lonsdale, Middleton and Sedbergh, although the latter is not easily seen. Sedbergh's former goods yard is more accessible, and still retains its original weigh office (with 1930s' weighbridge) and goods shed, plus a later provender store.

Conclusion

Two scenes from the photographs used for this book give clues as to the rise and fall of passenger rail services in Cumbria. The opening ceremony for Brampton Town station's NER services shows Lady Cecilia Roberts unlocking the gate with a silver key, attended by other local landowners, an MP, and a director of the NER presiding over the ceremony. Elsewhere the Town Band performed, and there were flags, bunting and banners, one reading 'Success to the Brampton Branch Railway'! A very different scene is shown for the start of Lowca's 'ordinary' passenger services. Here only railway staff pose by the locomotive, with a small crowd of working people on the tracks and single platform. In the background is Lowca No. 10 colliery, which, with its washery, kept the line open until 1973, long after the end of passenger services.

Yet, despite the obvious differences, there are marked similarities between the occasions and their railway lines. For a start they are almost contemporary, separated by less than two months in 1913. Both mark the addition of passenger services to lines previously used for freight (although Brampton's was the third attempt at this). Neither lasted long; Brampton's services, even with a three-year break for the First World War, ended in 1923, Lowca's three years later. Lastly and crucially both were solely to meet local demands, once these fell away both services were doomed.

This is one of two key elements in the demise of Cumbrian railways. In the vast majority of cases they were only of local importance, with just the 'Waverley Route' north of Carlisle amongst the closed lines having any national significance. The other element is their dependence on freight, especially the movement of minerals. Few of the closed lines were built primarily for passenger traffic, even where this later became important; for example the lines to Coniston and Keswick, often thought of as 'tourist' lines, were built for the movement of copper ore, and iron ore plus coke, respectively. In West Cumbria the dominance of freight was total, and in most cases passenger-carrying, as at Lowca, was only added later and on a very limited basis.

These two factors, the local nature of the lines and their dependence on mineral traffic, help explain the early end of passenger services in many areas of Cumbria. Once mines and iron works closed as the area went into economic decline, and local bus services took away the passengers, few lines were able to survive. Of the 24 lines listed on the 'Dates of Opening and Final Closure to Regular Passenger Traffic' page, over half had closed to passengers by the start of the Second World War, with a further six by the time of 'Beeching'. Only a final five were closures as a result of the Beeching Report, although that document did recommend closure of the Settle & Carlisle Railway and the coast line between Barrow and Whitehaven. Fortunately those two have survived, along with the West Coast Main Line, and the lines between Carnforth and Barrow, Whitehaven and Carlisle, and Carlisle and Newcastle, plus the three preserved railways featured in the book, to give some working lines amongst the 'lost railways' of Cumbria. As this book has shown, there are stretches of disused line that can be walked, both in the hills and near the coast, along with former stations, tunnels and viaducts to be viewed, as evidence of the once extensive network in this area. Even with their out-of-the-way location and often limited passenger operations, the 'Lost Railways of Cumbria' have left a significant legacy that can still be sampled today.

Opening and Final Closure Dates of Lines to Regular Passenger Traffic

Line	Opened	Final Closure
Brampton branch	15.7.1836	29.10.1923
Piel branch	24.8.1846	6.7.1936
Workington–Cockermouth	28.4.1847	18.4.1966
Port Carlisle branch	22.6.1854	1.6.1932[2]
Drumburgh–Silloth	28.8.1856	7.9.1964
Foxfield–Coniston	18.6.1859[1]	6.10.1958
Barnard Castle–Tebay (Stainmore)	8.8.1861	22.1.1962[3]
Low Gill–Clapham	16.9.1861[1]	1.2.1954
Kirkby Stephen–Penrith	7.6.1862	22.1.1962
Carlisle–Edinburgh (Waverley Route)	1.7.1862[1]	6.1.1969
Cockermouth–Penrith	2.1.1865	6.3.1972[4]
Moor Row–Marron Junction	2.4.1866	13.4.1931
Aspatria–Mealsgate[5]	26.12.1866	22.9.1930
Derwent branch	1.6.1867	29.4.1935
Plumpton Junction–Lake Side	1.6.1869	6.9.1965[6]
Mirehouse Junction–Sellafield	2.8.1869[1]	16.6.1947
Solway Junction Railway	2.8.1870	20.5.1921
Arnside–Hincaster Junction	26.6.1876	4.5.1942
Cleator Moor–Siddick Junction	1.9.1880[1]	13.4.1931

Distington–Parton	1.6.1881	1.9.1914
Conishead Priory branch	27.6.1883	1.1.1917
Distington–Oatlands[7]	3.7.1883	Sep 1922
Calva Junction–Seaton[8]	4.1.1888	Feb 1922
Harrington & Lowca Light Railway	2.6.1913	31.5.1926

Note: Closure dates are those posted by the operating company, usually a Monday, with the last train on the previous Saturday or Sunday. Reopenings by preservation societies have not been included.

[1] Opened in stages to this date

[2] East of Drumburgh the line continued in use for Silloth trains until 7.9.1964

[3] Tebay–Kirkby Stephen closed 1.12.1952

[4] Cockermouth–Keswick closed 18.4.1966

[5] East of Mealsgate there were services to Wigton 1877–1921

[6] Partly reopened by the Lakeside & Haverthwaite Railway in 1973

[7] Passenger services extended to Arlecdon 1912–1916

[8] Passenger services extended to Linefoot Sept–Nov 1908

Bibliography

Many of the following are out of print but can still be obtained second-hand or consulted in libraries.

Bowtell, Harold D. *Rails Through Lakeland** [Workington/Cockermouth/Keswick/Penrith] (Silver Link Publishing)

Caplan, Neil *The Waverley Route* (Ian Allan)

Davies W.J.K. *Ravenglass & Eskdale Railway* (originally published by David & Charles and reissued by Atlantic Publishing)

Edgar, Stuart & Sinton, John M. *The Solway Junction Railway* (Oakwood Press)

Gradon, William McGowan *The Track of the Ironmasters* [Cleator & Workington Junction Railway] (originally published by the author and reissued by the Cumbrian Railways Association)

Hoole, K. *The Stainmore Railway* (Dalesman Books)

Joy, David *Cumbrian Coast Railways* (Dalesman Books)

Joy, David *The Lake Counties* (volume 14 in the 'Regional History of the Railways of Great Britain' series published by David & Charles)

Marshall, John *Forgotten Railways: North West England* (David & Charles)

Mullay, A.J. *Rails Across the Border* (Patrick Stephens)

Norman, K.J. *The Furness Railway**(Silver Link Publishing)

Quayle, Howard & Jenkins, Stanley *The Lakeside & Haverthwaite Railway* (Dalesman Books)

Simmons, Jack *The Maryport & Carlisle Railway* (Oakwood Press)

Webb, Brian & Gordon, David A. *Lord Carlisle's Railways* [includes the Brampton branch] (Railway Travel & Correspondence Society)

Western, Robert *The Coniston Branch* (Oakwood Press)

Western, Robert *The Ingleton Branch* [originally published as *The Lowgill Branch*] (Oakwood Press)

White, Stephen *Solway Steam* [Port Carlisle and Silloth lines] (Carel Press, Carlisle)

* Both of these were originally published as single volumes and later reissued as two-volume editions.

A particularly useful website for parts of this area is at: www.cumbria-railways.co.uk

Index